The
Weekender
Effect II

The Weekender Effect II

Fallout

ROBERT WILLIAM SANDFORD

RMB
rmbooks.com

Sections of this book were published in earlier publications. Parts of the Prologue and the sections on what defines sense of place, though altered, are borrowed from *The Weekender Effect: Hyperdevelopment in Mountain Towns*. Parts of "Backstory: Shot Out of a Cold Cannon" were in *Our Vanishing Glaciers: The Snows of Yesteryear and the Future Climate of the Mountain West*. The section on Wallace Stegner's influence was first published in Stephen Legault's *Imagine This Valley: Essays and Stories Celebrating the Bow Valley*. Parts of "Backstory: What We Saved Could Now Save Us" were originally published in *Ecology & Wonder in the Canadian Rocky Mountain Parks World Heritage Site*.

For information on purchasing bulk quantities of this book, or to obtain media excerpts or invite the author to speak at an event, please visit rmbooks.com and select the "Contact" tab.

RMB | Rocky Mountain Books Ltd.
rmbooks.com
@rmbooks
facebook.com/rmbooks

Cataloguing data available from Library and Archives Canada
ISBN 9781771606080 (softcover)
ISBN 9781771606097 (electronic)

Printed and bound in Canada

We would like to also take this opportunity to acknowledge the traditional territories upon which we live and work. In Calgary, Alberta, we acknowledge the Niitsitapi (Blackfoot) and the people of the Treaty 7 region in Southern Alberta, which includes the Siksika, the Piikuni, the Kainai, the Tsuut'ina, and the Stoney Nakoda First Nations, including Chiniki, Bearpaw, and Wesley First Nations. The City of Calgary is also home to Métis Nation of Alberta, Region III. In Victoria, British Columbia, we acknowledge the traditional territories of the Lkwungen (Esquimalt and Songhees), Malahat, Pacheedaht, Scia'new, T'Sou-ke, and W̱SÁNEĆ (Pauquachin, Tsartlip, Tsawout, Tseycum) peoples.

We acknowledge the financial support of the Government of Canada through the Canada Book Fund and the Canada Council for the Arts, and of the province of British Columbia through the British Columbia Arts Council and the Book Publishing Tax Credit.

Disclaimer
The views expressed in this book are those of the author and do not necessarily reflect those of the publishing company, its staff, or its affiliates.

For our children

The question, then, is not so much how to create the world as how to keep alive that moment of creation, how to realize the Coyote world in which creation never ends and people participate in the power of being creators, a world whose hopefulness lies in its unfinishedness, its openness to improvisation and participation. The revolutionary days I have been outlining are days in which hope is no longer fixed in the future: it becomes an electrifying force in the present.

—Rebecca Solnit, *Hope in the Dark: Untold Histories, Wild Possibilities*

Contents

Contents

Invocation

I have had a falling out with the place in which I have chosen to live for most of my adult life; the people and the place that has meant the most to me of any place on Earth; the place I have helped build; the place I have defended and celebrated and believed in; the place I have loved.

I don't know what happened to my deep connection to where I live; to my abiding sense of place; to my confidence in it and its future. Where once I wore my passion for where I live on my sleeve, I now have to work to evoke it, as if it has become vestigial, something I had inside me that slowly withered, rather like the appendix has done over time in the human body.

I have lost my place, so to speak. How could I have allowed this to happen?

How did I allow my spirit to drain out of me? Why did I allow myself to become a ghost? Was it a wrong turn I took on the greater highway of life, or did I catch a low-level infection that gradually suppressed the spirit of place within me in the way COVID-19 suppressed taste and smell? Or did the deafening proliferation of social media drivel drown it out?

Or is it that I can't feel it anymore because it has been trampled out of shape by the hordes of pilgrims that now stomp in their ski boots and golf spikes and ride their mountain bikes at speed through the temple of time that was once mine to enter, each seeking evidently the experience – or something like it – of the sublime in our landscapes and our selves that I once cherished as sacred?

Or has my sense of place become vestigial because I have surrendered my sacred places to these hordes?

Or is it that over the past two decades so much has changed that I barely recognize the community in which I live, or, more accurately, the community in which I used to live?

Was it because I wasn't paying enough attention that, while I wasn't looking, where I live became a weekend retreat and retirement village for the world's rich? Or is it because it appears that in terms of further development, we can expect more of the same in the coming decade? Evidently, we haven't seen anything yet. It appears at the time of this writing that, if outside developers have their way – and it appears inevitable that in one way or another they will – this once small and quaint mountain town, which has already grown by 500 per cent since I moved here, will have added another 10,000 mostly weekenders to its population. In other words, unless your goal is to make more money trafficking on the former local character of the town and its spectacular surroundings and you don't care about community or the living landscapes that surround it and define that character, nothing is going to get better.

Whatever the reasons for all this rapid change, this fallout presents a problem if you have a deep connection to place. What happens when the place in which you live becomes commodified and urbanized to the extent that you begin to feel displaced? What happens when where you live starts to push you out, to alienate you? What happens when where you live, and most of the people among whom you are forced to live, begin to disgust you? How does one manage the growing sense that you are becoming a refugee under self-imposed house arrest in the place you have lived and loved most of your life?

When that happens, it may be time to confront your situation and your feelings. The mountains in which I live have for all of my productive life been the centre of my being. This, I should point out, has nothing to do with religion, which, having been exposed to the injustice it has wrought here and elsewhere in the world, I abhor. What I am talking about here, however, is unquestionably spiritual; it is about how one's own spirit can resonate with the spirit of place in ways that over time deeply define personal authenticity and local identity.

We are increasingly denying ourselves meaningful access to the places of natural power we once counted upon to renew our connection with the indwelling spirits of the landscapes among which we live. There are now, among the most sacred of local places, some you can't even get to for the hordes. In such circumstances, we are distracted away from the humbling timelessness of the peaks, and the exquisite and ephemeral beauty of iconic mountain lakes. The sacred becomes merely a backdrop. What takes centre stage are the hordes themselves. Nearby Lake Louise, for example, over the ever-lengthening tourist season is little more than a midway attraction. The same thing has happened at Moraine

Lake. And as the congestion has grown it has also spread beyond the boundaries of popular nearby national parks. The hordes have now arrived in such numbers at Grassi Lakes and other local places of concentrated natural power where I live that we had to close them for a summer to greatly expand the parking capacity at their trailheads.

If this is what is happening here, what is happening in other mountain towns and resort communities facing the same pressures? We know the answer to that question. As outsider interests seek to appropriate the last best places in the interests of real estate speculation and personal prestige, local people are increasingly facing dispossession. Many are finding they can no longer afford to live – and often don't want to continue to live – in the places in which they created the unique character of community and deep sense of place that eventually made them so pleasant to live in and visit that their very attractiveness led to their being changed almost beyond recognition. And when those people are pushed out, when those people leave, wherever they go they cannot help but become the problem that they sought to escape.

That this infection has spread to almost all of the world's accessible places of great cultural significance or natural beauty demands a broader than local assessment of the direction that these trends will take us in the future.

Some observers – mostly academics – continue to maintain that this is simply "amenity migration," the inevitable gravitation of wealth to the most exclusive places. Others argue that we should expect this as part of the price of globalization and the increasing homogenization of global culture. For some, it suggests an even broader possibility. Might it be possible for one to have a deep connection, not just with one specific adopted geography or culture, but with the entire planet? An Earth belonging, so to speak.

Is it possible that there can be more than one place in the world where we can feel we truly belong? Or is it the case that when the curse of cultural homogenization and global real estate speculation makes more and more of the last best places the same, equally unafford-able for most, and all equally shallow in terms of community and local culture, that the lights will go out in each? Or will we find the world we appear to be about to inherit is in no way a substitute for the one we lost?

In the faces of forces like these, I am forced to ask myself how I, and others like me, can hang on to where we live. How do I prevent myself and my deepest connections to the living world from being swept away by all this? If it is still inside me, can I – in the wake of the COVID-19 pandemic – restore my sense and love of place and live by and through it as I once did?

Can I keep my place, so to speak, so that when my ashes are spread among these peaks, I will at last and eternally be one with them?

This book attempts to answer to those questions.

Prologue

What's past is prologue.
—William Shakespeare

In 2008, I wrote a small book called *The Weekender Effect: Hyperdevelopment in Mountain Towns*. The book was published by Rocky Mountain Books as the first volume in their "manifesto series" of short, concise and well-informed books on matters related to environment and culture. The book, as is so often the case with books, was inspired by a chance encounter with prospective new neighbours who had evidently moved in down the street in Canmore, Alberta, where I live.

I will never forget the encounter. The door-bell rang and I opened it to find a well-dressed middle-aged couple standing before me. They introduced themselves as the people who had just bought a house a few doors down on the quiet street on which we live. They were quick to tell us that they were from Toronto, and that he was a very successful management consultant who worked widely in the world. The man's wife then posed an interesting question: Did we live here full time? At that point in my life, I couldn't afford living anywhere except full time, so I responded that, indeed, yes, by that time for more than 15 years. Her second question was the one that floored me and which led me ultimately to writing *The Weekender Effect*. She looked at me, mysti-fied, and said, "You mean you only have one house?" As at that time I could barely imagine having one house, the question astounded me. "As a matter of fact," I said, "we are poor and I am afraid that this is the only house we have." The couple looked very disappointed, as if they hadn't counted on living on a street with people who were not their economic and social peers. How could they possibly explain to their friends that some of their neighbours were so down and out they only had one house? They then quickly excused themselves and scampered off down the street, having already decided, I'm sure, that we were not the class of people with whom they wanted to associate. And, of course, we never saw them again.

At first, I laughed it off, but the more I started to look into what was happening to our town the less I found anything to laugh about. The town was under invasion from the outside, and if locals didn't wake up to what was happening and see what we ourselves were doing to our own community by virtue of our short-sightedness, we would soon arrive at circumstances in which all but the most cunning among us found ourselves encountering dispossession.

My first concern, as I noted in the invocation, was that the people who established the unique community character of the town would increasingly find they could no longer afford to live here and, worse, that the place had changed so much from what they wanted their town to be that they no longer had any reason or incentive to stay. The deeper I looked, however, the more troubling were my findings.

I found there was a pattern to the behaviour of those who found themselves increasingly dispossessed by the rapid outside transformation of the town in which they lived. There was often a step-like progression to dispossession. You enjoy going out every day, but gradually you start seeing the increased traffic congestion and crowding and seeing more people doing things that disrespect place as you have come to know it. On top of this, stack a growing sense of environmental grief as it becomes more and more clear that we are causing the entire biodiversity-based Earth system to unravel.

Despair over diminishment and loss grows in you. You go out fewer days, and then fewer and fewer days, until you begin to feel that where you live has been suddenly occupied by an invading force. Gradually, you don't want to go out. Then you lose faith in place and stop going out. Then you wake up one morning and you don't want to live where you live anymore.

As one would expect, there were two very polarized responses to the book. People I didn't know were not the least bit shy to approach me at public events and stab me in the sternum with a chubby index finger and grunt out how much they hated my book. This happened frequently enough that I formulated a polite response. "No problem," I said. "May I propose that if you didn't like my book about development in mountain towns that you write your own?" No one has come forward, at least at the time of this writing in response. From this I have surmised that either outside developers and anonymous foreign real estate speculators are too busy making money to worry about how they are perceived in the court of local public opinion, or maybe they just don't write books.

Not much has changed in that regard since I wrote *The Weekender Effect*. The fact is that development interests don't need to appear in the court of public opinion, where they might be mocked or criticized by an informed citizenry for their lack of sensitivity to or understanding of environmental issues and their wilful blindness regarding what matters to those who actually live in the community as opposed to those who occupy space and use up land that could become precious affordable housing, making it impossible for many to live here. Why should they care anyway? Other courts protect and advance their interests.

The second common reaction against what I said in *The Weekender Effect* was more predictable. If I so disliked living here, why didn't I just get up and leave? At the time my response to that question was much the same as it is now,

15 years later as I write this sequel. Leaving here for British Columbia, say, would be tantamount to giving in to the mean-spirited and highly divisive populist who at the time of this writing was the premier of Alberta and caving in to the largest majority of selfish, feckless "hatriots" who voted him in. I know I live here among these people, but that does not mean I have to give in morally or grant their organized "hatriarchy" any legitimacy. In other words, I refuse to give in to self-exile. If I do leave here, I want to do so on my own terms – preferably in a pine box – which should suggest I will do everything possible to prevent becoming the problem elsewhere should I escape from here.

I realize now that there are some things I got wrong in *The Weekender Effect*. The first big thing I got wrong is that I completely underestimated the contribution that many weekenders and retirees would make to the positive development and evolution of the community.

Many of these people brought exceptional skills and a broad range of often very specialized experience and competence with them, which they have generously offered to the community.

The first people who come to mind here are the doctors and health care professionals we have attracted by way of quality of life to this community. They are among the very best in the world, and provide comprehensive health care far beyond what one could reasonably expect, at least in a community of our current size. We are lucky to have them here.

But there are also many others who started as weekenders who have moved here with their families and now do all they can to add value to the community. They include many Americans, some clearly part of the first wave of climate migrants coming from the United States. They also include professors we have attracted from the most prestigious climate research institutions in the United States and the researchers they in turn have attracted from all over the world. They now work at what has become one of the leading water research laboratories in the country in Canmore.

What I also missed was the potential emergence of whole neighbourhoods of these people who are now reaffirming community values on their own unique terms on the streets where they live.

I should point out that it was never my intention to suggest there weren't good people and responsible citizens who contribute to a naturally evolving sense of place. The problem is that there are too many of them, they arrived in greater numbers than we could absorb into the community, and too many of them want too much.

What I also did not anticipate was just how deeply persistent sense of place would remain in many of the people who have resisted being overwhelmed by change in this town and this valley. There remain here a great many people –

famous mountaineers, Olympic skiers and adventurers, as well as ordinary hikers and birdwatchers, whose lives outside their daily work have been shaped by their experience of place and who refuse to have it any other way.

Another thing I missed was the deep compassion that many here had for disadvantaged others, an example of which I recently witnessed when nearly the entire town came together to express their deep and sincere support for the neuro-diverse community that lives among us, whom they celebrated. "I am different, yes, but I am not less" was the message all shared. "Together, we can make a difference" was the group's motto. And they already have.

Another thing I got wrong is that I underestimated the power of this landscape to inspire artists, musicians, writers and filmmakers. The town's successful public art program has resulted in the work of resident artists with national reputations being exhibited widely in the community.

Then there is music. Sully's Garage, the Elektric Squirrels, Vi's Guys and, of course, the world-class annual Canmore Folk Music Festival. In the tradition of the Pine Tree Players, theatre culture is still vibrant here, and the new artsPlace now offers movies as well as regular art exhibitions.

And what does it mean to have one of the highest per capita number of poets and writers in a place? And so many readers? And one of the best independent bookstores in the country? It means a great deal.

But there are some things in *The Weekender Effect* that, judging from what has happened in the 15 years since I wrote it, I did not get wrong. Many of the people who live here have little reason to live here, at least in terms of deep and meaningful connection to the place itself. The COVID-19 pandemic, and the pressure to work in a comfortable setting wherever you choose to work, accelerated this trend. Many among this influx may have some feeling for the mountains as backdrop, but they have little connection to the vast region in which they live, and only a fledgling sense of mountain place. For many it is the prestige of having a second or third home in a tony mountain town. For a great many others, it is merely a good, solid speculative investment. This could all change, perhaps, if federal law prohibited foreign home sales or if the community decided to create a campaign to encourage newcomers to better understand and honour local values and to adopt them. This would, however, take time, and the contest over the soul of the community is happening now. In the context of the Town's "Mining the Future" public engagement exercise, there are too many here who are literally commodifying and then mining the landscape and the value of place, which is exactly what we didn't want. This has had unforeseen consequences.

Besides sheer population numbers, perhaps the biggest changes since I moved here reside in growing wealth disparity and increasing traffic.

Since I wrote *The Weekender Effect* the gap between those who have a great deal and those who have far, far less has grown exponentially. Many more people here are now house-rich and lifestyle-poor. In addition, there is a lot less place to have a sense of, and fewer and fewer locals have the abundant time they once had to pursue a deep, personal sense of a mountain landscape that weekenders and outside others appear to be turning into a gymnasium for mechanized sports. COVID only intensified these trends, which in turn increased our vulnerability to further diminishment and loss.

It can no longer be denied that by commodifying place and dramatically increasing the wealth disparity among its citizenry, we are indeed diminishing where we live. By pushing the ecological limits of where we live, developing every possible empty space and eliminating affordable housing that could be occupied by locals who genuinely want to live here for authentic reasons related to their own identity but cannot afford even one house here, we are robbing ourselves of true community. And we are not done yet. At full build-out to the extent outside developers have proposed there will be precious little montane habitat and even less room for wildlife. As many of us here are here because we can share our lives with other forms of life, there are not only bound to be – there should be and already are – tensions. And yet we remain largely oblivious to how lucky we are. Most of the rest of the world would give anything to have what we are giving up – what we are, in effect, squandering.

Since I wrote *The Weekender Effect*, I've begun to work directly with the United Nations. That work has taken me to many countries, many of them failed or near-failed states. Such places do not have resources we take for granted. It is heartbreaking to try to help when communities are collapsing in the absence of even the most basic safety nets, creating situations in which people have begun to act in desperation to save themselves and their families. When I come back from the real world I cannot but be stunned by the sense of privilege and entitlement that are the everyday norm here. Compared to other places in the world, we have almost no sense of what our stability and our security are worth and how easily they can be lost.

And then, suddenly, along came the pandemic to shatter all that.

At first it seemed that slowing down for a time wasn't necessarily going to be a bad thing. There is an old saying that if you can't fish, then spend the time mending your nets. The pandemic rattled us and it rattled on. We were forced to pause and take stock of ourselves. Who are we? Who do we want to be?

I saw in this enforced pause huge potential opportunity. Perhaps this might be turned into a transformational moment, the one many have been waiting for – the moment when we could finally stop going down the wrong path and head again in the direction of creating a culture worthy of the astounding landscapes in which we live. Perhaps, in this moment of hiatus, we could create a culture commensurate with place.

I thought the pandemic might put our inflated sense of individual privilege and entitlement into relief. While that hasn't happened – at least not yet – lots else did. We found we are in a long game with COVID. We can't beat ourselves up for what we didn't know about our opponent or for how uncertainly we played. It is a home game, however, and we can't forfeit. Though the game is far from over at the time of this writing, we are lucky the COVID score wasn't higher. There is much, however, that we can and should learn from it.

In a way, our reaction to COVID is like our reaction to community and place. The integrity and our resilience as a community is defined by the values and collective behaviour of all around us. The premise of this book is that we need to re-examine our values and collective behaviour as a coherent mountain community before it is too late to prevent the deterioration of the landscapes and the landscape experiences upon which we depend for what constitutes our *real* prosperity: the potential all of us – locals and newcomers alike – possess for deep, respectful and enduring connection to the place and to one another, a connection that will be vital to our survival in the face of a rapidly changing outside world.

The Backstory

The Stage Is Set

Every story has a backstory, the story behind the story, so to speak. There is a backstory behind this book. Please permit me to tell it to you, but as I do, I hope you will reflect on your own story of how you became connected to where you live.

The fact is that I did not always possess a deep sense of connection with the Earth. In fact, when I started out I barely had any connection at all. I grew up in a downtown neighbourhood in a prairie city. As I remember, the extent of my connection to the natural world was limited to raking the leaves of the single cottonwood poplar that grew in our yard. It wasn't until I was 9 that I actually witnessed a prairie sunrise.

I remember it well. I was driving with my older sister and her husband to a wedding in Medicine Hat when a huge yellow ball rose above the endless horizon before us. I asked my brother-in-law, who was driving while the rest of us slept, what that extraordinary orb could be. "It's the sun," he said, without so much as a hint of astonishment that I had never seen such a thing. "It's the sun rising." I vowed to never forget him or that summer morning.

As I grew up, I took an interest in biology. It wasn't long until I decided that what I wanted to be when I grew up was a doctor. But, according to my high school teachers, I wasn't cut out to be a doctor. My grades were simply not good enough to ever get into medical school. But my biology teacher, Mr. Berndt, told me there was much I could do if I chose to become a biologist. He then went on to help me see the wide potential that existed for someone who had an interest in the life sciences. I vowed never to forget him either.

The first two years of university were glorious. I was presented with as much as I could possibly absorb and much that I still remember. I was intellectually on fire, and I wanted to stay that way.

Though I loved the natural sciences, I found myself gravitating toward paleo-history. At the end of the second year of university, I applied to go on an archaeology field school in Guatemala. Unfortunately, however, this was at the time of the beginning of the troubles in Guatemala. The West German ambassador was killed in Guatemala City, and, as hostilities intensified, it was soon deemed too dangerous for foreigners to visit the country. The field school was cancelled. I was desolate. It was late April and I had no prospects for a desperately needed summer job.

Then, out of the blue, there came a phone call. It was from what was then known as the National Parks Service of Canada. It took me a few moments to understand why I had been called. I had almost forgotten that a few weeks earlier, though I didn't think I was qualified, I had applied at the university employment centre on a competition for the job of what was then called a seasonal park naturalist. The woman on the other end of the phone clearly knew that I wasn't qualified either. She prefaced the job offer she put before me by saying, "While you were not our first choice..." and she offered me a three-month summer position as a park naturalist in nearby Banff National Park. I ignored for the moment that I didn't know the difference between a goat and mountain sheep, between a wolf and a coyote, or even between a Canadian beaver and a muskrat, and gratefully accepted the job.

It was – and I should say never ceases to be – a steep learning curve. I vowed to never forget those first few weeks of training. I never want to forget the state of sheer awe in which I remained suspended living in and surrounded by so much natural splendour. I felt it my duty to always remember clearly how experiencing places like Moraine Lake or Peyto Lake Viewpoint for the first time so took my breath away, for if I could keep these memories alive and close at hand, I would know and be able to empathize fully with what first-time visitors were experiencing. I could be a reliable bridge between them and not just their experience of our national parks but a connection to all of the living Earth they could take home with them and further cultivate where they lived. Everyone around me seemed to have the same goal, and we fed on each other's astonishment and joy. I have that same goal still.

The legendary Banff historian, philosopher and poet Jon Whyte once mused that discovering where you belong can be a powerful "born again" experience not unlike what "born again" Christians claim to have in at last finding faith. What Jon was describing, however, was not a denominationally religious revelation but a personal spiritual transformation brought about by encounters with the powers of place – that is, provided you survive them.

We all have stories about how we come to find home. I am surprised sometimes by how many such stories involve water, or I should say more accurately, accidents on water: adventures on big lakes, unexpected storms, tipped canoes, falling through lake ice, near drownings. If one weren't careful, a full inventory of such occurrences might suggest we are, in essence, a water nation. If one were to undertake such an inventory, one might also discover that many of these life-altering experiences were the product of inexperience and nearly complete incompetence and that the transcendence born of them could only be attributed to youthful good luck. My story is certainly among the latter.

As I have written elsewhere, I think it is fair to say that I have an intimate connection to at least one river – the Saskatchewan. It is fair to say also that I came to know the Saskatchewan quite by accident.

The story is worth retelling in this sequel because of the Doppler effect of history, even if that history is of your own life. The events that shape one's identity take on different dimensions and new meanings as time passes and one heaps new experiences and perspectives upon one's personal creation story.

Like so many who come to work in the Rockies, I was young: 20 years old. You may not remember being 20, but if you do, you may remember it as an exciting but uncertain period of your life. Unlike most of my

20-year-old friends, I had my life all worked out. I was going to graduate. I had picked a wife. I had picked a house. There would be a dog. There would be children. I would drive a wood-panelled station wagon. If you are old enough to remember what a wood-panelled station wagon looked like, you will recognize that I was prepared, indeed, for the good life. Then I fell unroped into a crevasse on the Saskatchewan Glacier.

The story is still told to disbelieving tourists. Imagine this. A person actually disappeared beneath the surface of ice and was washed through a glacier to come out its snout. Even if you hadn't ever seen a glacier, such a story would sound far-fetched, like one of the whoppers some group tour drivers tell their passengers on the famous Icefields Parkway on the way, perhaps, to see a real glacier. The fact remains that this story is true.

Like all of our personal disasters, it all began innocently enough. After viewing a dazzling array of mountain climbing photographs projected on the wall by friends of the fellow naturalist with whom I lived at a warden station on the Icefields Parkway, I decided I wanted to become a mountaineer. Even though I had no experience whatsoever, and had never even backpacked in my life, there was of course no point in half measures. The first backpacking trip I did in my entire life was across the largest glacier pouring down from the Columbia Icefield, with the aim of going to what were almost mythically known as the Castleguard Meadows.

Even though I had seen the glacier many times from the top of a neighbouring ridge and already told many visitors of its exact dimensions, I still had no practical idea of the challenges an ice mass on that scale might pose in terms of the time, energy and basic skill that would be required to climb and then descend it. I only had two days off, but that, in my opinion and in the opinion of the much more experienced others I was to join on the trip, ought to have been enough. After all, when you are 20, how big can a glacier be?

The accident happened while we were descending the Saskatchewan Glacier on the afternoon of the second day. We were unroped and the experienced climber I was with was far ahead of me. I was so tired that I had given up trying to avoid the big meltwater streams that coursed across the glacier's broken surface. I was cold and wet and worn out and all I wanted to do was get down. So I did what people with no experience might do. I took a shortcut.

Unless you have travelled on the surface of a big glacier, it is hard to imagine how much melt can occur on a hot day. There are actually rivers on the surface of the ice. Seeking a direct line, I tried to cross one, not knowing that moving water over ice polishes that ice to the consistency of glass.

The power of the icy water lifted me up and carried me to the mouth of a huge crevasse.

One moment I was looking at the sun-sparkle of splashing water; a moment later I was in the centre of waterfall plunging into complete darkness beneath the ice.

The waterfall cascaded down a series of ice lips to join the river that flowed beneath the glacier. In only moments I caught up with and passed underneath my astonished companion, who had seen me go down. Never before or since have I heard from everywhere around me so many of the different sounds that water makes. Here I was inside a planetary artery examining first-hand what water does to the world. But then I had a problem.

Only a few inches separated the top of the water and the roof of the ice. In darkness, I kept smashing into boulders and scraping against the underside of the glacier. But, just as the shock and wonder were beginning to evaporate, just as calm was about to become sheer terror, the strangest thing happened.

The ice above began to glow.

At first it was a faint green. As the river swept me onward the glow intensified. Green gradually merged into a pale blue. I then noticed rocks suspended in a ceiling made entirely of light.

Then I washed out of the glacier into sunshine and into the full flood of the North Saskatchewan River, where my problems really began.

While I didn't realize it at the time, that was the end of my life as I had anticipated living it. The accident changed everything. My life flowed toward unexpected ends. I never did get that wood-panelled Ford. Though I did get a dog, it wasn't till years later that I married the wife of my dreams.

I realize now that I have spent the rest of my life trying to prevent my own culture from carrying me permanently downstream and away from the luminous glory of that subglacial light.

The accident taught me that the relationship between people and the places in which they live is a complicated one.

For the first weeks after the accident, I remained in terror of the mountains. Just being in them gave me the shakes. I was given a temporary leave and returned home to Calgary, where the first stages of the transformation slowly unfolded. Being in the city grated on me. I had trouble sleeping. After a week, I started to get up before dawn to drive out onto the prairies to watch the sun rise. I suddenly discovered where I came from.

Then, as if a deep connection to one place allows deep connections to develop within one to other places, the strangest thing happened. Gradually, instead of being terrified of going back to the mountains, I was drawn to them. And once I returned, I felt as entirely different in their presence as I felt different about myself. The peaks had not changed, but they had changed me. I saw in them now not just their breathtaking splendour but also their terrible beauty. Awe was now married to deep respect and a need to know how to live safely, if only relatively briefly, among them and learn their wisdom. There was something in them and in myself I needed to learn. I was a smallness in something so much larger. I was an infinitesimal and fleeting presence trying to contemplate the nature of an infinitely larger living presence within which I was living and that I now had to explore. At the end of the summer, I didn't want to leave.

When I went back to university, things did not go well. While I had a huge appetite for learning, I couldn't concentrate. Because the National Parks Service paid well for summer jobs, I could now afford a car. Drawn by something inside me I could not ignore, I started skipping classes to spend days at a time in the mountains. I wanted to know everything about them: the defining feature of every rock stratum; the names and histories of every tree and flower; and the identities and habits of every creature that lived in or within sight of the peaks. And, because I didn't want to die pursuing these understandings, I especially wanted to know about mountain hazards.

As I spent subsequent summers working in the same job, I gradually gravitated toward the environmental movement, not necessarily because I wanted to, but because for me at the time it was the only church in town.

In time I developed the righteousness of the devout but soon realized that this righteousness was not always an asset and that if I pursued and deepened it, it would not be long until the only people I could talk to and would listen to me would be people who belonged to the same church. I wearied of the confessions I had to make. I also got tired of the self-proclaimed high priests and over-zealous church elders telling me what to think, what to do and how much to put into the collection plate.

That the environmental movement was beginning to resemble a political party became impossible to ignore. I decided I didn't want my deepening personal connection with place to become politicized. While I greatly admired and still admire many of these people for their commitment to environmental and social justice, and found the intentions of the movement noble, I did not want to be subsumed within it and just become one of the congregation. By that time, I had been living in the mountains long enough to feel that they were the place I knew best and the only place that seemed to know me in return. I felt I had to find my own way. To have an impact that extended beyond singing to the church choir, I had to follow my own path, which meant I had to define my own relationship with the forces that shaped the landscapes that meant so much to me. Only this way could I hope to help further inspire the perpetuation of a culture truly commensurate with the remarkable character of place in the community in which I had by then come to live. And that, fortunately, is when I discovered Wallace Stegner.

Wallace Stegner

I forgive Wallace Stegner for being an American because, in fact, he grew up in southern Saskatchewan and returned there 40 years later to write the definitive book on sense of place on the prairies, called *Wolf Willow*.

In *Wolf Willow*, and other books such as *The American West as Living Space*, *The Sound of Mountain Water*, *Angle of Repose* and *Where the Bluebird Sings at Lemonade Springs*, Stegner attempted to define the elements of the nostalgia created in our own minds by the landscapes in which we live, which he called "a sense of place."

Stegner's specific gift to me was a clear definition of the steps that might take one in the direction of how I had begun to perceive the unique relationship to landscape and culture that was driving my own deepening connection to place.

Though American and Canadian writers and critics have attempted to enlarge his categories somewhat, those remain, in effect, as he articulated them. Sense of place, as defined by Stegner, was composed of three essential elements.

The first is unique geography. A person could only appreciate a sense of place where they lived if they saw the geography of where they lived as special. As I have said so often, it is hard not to feel that way here. The geography of the Rockies leans in on you, it is hard to ignore. Even unseen in darkness and storm, the mountains exert a presence. This presence is sometimes subtle, but it can be profound. Often people don't know the physical landscape is reaching into them and making them locals, by gradual association if not by choice.

The second element of place is a remembered and celebrated history. This history is most often personal or family in nature. You have to have a history in that place. Perhaps you remember the first time you were overtaken by the smell of pines. Or perhaps you recall the excitement and fear that accompanied your first encounter with a bear. You remember the stream where you caught your first fish.

What happened to you is as or more important than the fact that the place around you may have been an exploration route or the site of an early trading post or a particularly interesting section on an early railway line. History starts with us as individuals and then radiates outward toward others.

The third step in coming home to place is related to how personal history merges with the larger history of a community and region. It is the application of personal history to contemporary meaning. An informed sense of place requires that what happened in a given place in the past has meaning in the present.

In reaching this stage in the adoption of place, you suddenly see yourself as part of a continuum in the life and experience of the community in which you have chosen to live. You are part of that continuum and it is part of you. You see how you live reflected in where you live.

Suddenly geology and topography have relevance. Suddenly you see why 10,000 years of Indigenous presence matters. You understand the impact of the coming of the railway, not just on your community but on your life. You see history as a continuum that not only includes you but affects how you and your neighbours live in your time.

It did not take me long to recognize that the establishment of this relationship often requires the skilled storytelling of elders, or the informed and enthusiastic interpretation of archaeologists, historians, naturalists and artists.

It is in recognition of all of these people that I proposed in all the classes on place I taught to add a fourth element to Stegner's remarkable list. Every real place possesses a cast of genuine local characters. These are people steeped in the geography, history and meaning of place who become crystals around which aesthetics are articulated and passed on through time. It is these people who have made sacrifices that have made them truly worthy and utterly representative of where they live. The moment you meet them you want to be like them.

These are people of such unique character that you immediately want to emulate their sincerity and connection to what is truly meaningful about where and how they live. In these people, sense of place has become a form of grace. That, I told the locals to whom I was often invited to speak, is the kind of person I wanted each of them to become. When people meet you, I told them, I want them to want to emulate your sincerity and connection to place. I want their memories of you to be inseparable from the experience of place you shared with them.

But Stegner's influence did not stop with his prescriptions for establishing a unique and deep relationship with the landscapes in which you live. That was only the beginning.

The list of the writers Stegner taught or influenced reads like the *Who's Who* of contemporary American literature. The list includes writers of the calibre of Barry Lopez, Ivan Doig, Gretel Ehrlich, Rick Bass, David Rains Wallace and Robert Stone.

One of Stegner's favourites – and one of my favourite people of all time – was Terry Tempest Williams. Tempest Williams laments in her writing that our society is gradually teaching us to withhold our emotions in the face of the loss of so much that is meaningful in the world. She maintains that over time we have allowed ourselves to believe we should not care too deeply about what is important around us because we are going to lose it anyway. She argues that we have become so used to hoarding our feelings that we have become inured to diminishment and loss. We have become so numb that when a landscape that matters to us is bought, sold or developed, clear-cut or grazed to rubble, or a hawk is shot and hung up by its feet on a barbed wire fence, our hearts are not broken because we no longer risk having strong emotional feelings about these matters. What kind of impoverishment, she asks, is it to withhold emotion, to restrain our natural connection to place just to appease our fears? She argues that a man or woman who reins in their heart when the body sings desperately for connection is only inviting more isolation and greater ecological decline. She claims that our lack of intimacy with each other is in direct proportion to our lack of intimacy with the land. She claims we have taken our love inside and abandoned the wild. This is not the West Williams wants. It is not the West Stegner wanted either.

William Kittredge also paid attention to Wallace Stegner and throughout his writing life built on Stegner's notion of the need to create a culture commensurate with place. In this, Kittredge maintains that keeping our language is far more important than we may know. We have our own language in many parts of the mountain West. To preserve what is essential about where and how we live, we must preserve this language, for the loss of words can lead to the loss of the things those words stand for. The devaluation of words makes for the devaluation of the things words describe. With fewer words to describe the places that surround us, it becomes harder to justify saving them. As these places vanish from our direct experience, the need for a language to describe them vanishes as well. William Kittredge warns us that languages can decay and die. Once the language that people used to tell the story of who they are vanishes, sense of self can be lost. People can become less than they were.

In his writing, Wes Jackson has urged Westerners to become native to where they live. In order to preserve even the possibility of enduring sense of place, Jackson contends that we have to slow down our aimless, wandering pursuit of upward mobility at any cost and find a home, dig in and aim for some kind of enduring relationship with the ecological realities of the surrounding landscape. Jackson believes that we have to somehow reverse the Western frontier tradition of picking up and leaving the moment a place is no longer what we want it to be. We have to learn to stop running away. We have to stay and stand up for where we live. We have to have confidence in what we are and what we can become. In this period of great change we have to trust in the resilience of Western landscapes and Western people.

Stegner biographer Philip Fradkin reports, however, that of all the students who passed through Stegner's creative writing program at Stanford, Wendell Berry was by far his favourite. Their admiration for each other's work and principles, Fradkin reports, was sustained for 35 years.

Wendell Berry maintains that you can't know who you are unless you know where you are. Berry is troubled by the destructive precedent we've inherited on this continent. Berry believes that by the time creatures have reached the level of consciousness they should have become conscious of the larger creation and how they fit into it. The failure to achieve this consciousness, Berry believes, will in the end exact a terrible penalty. The spirit of the creation will go out of them, they will become destructive and then the very Earth will depart from them and go where they cannot follow.

At the age of 60 Stegner soured on conservation politics. The trouble started in his own backyard. In 1949 he and his wife Mary had built a home on seven acres of land in the Los Altos hills in what was then rural California, east of San Francisco. One morning, however, Wallace and Mary woke up to discover that where they lived was about to become Silicon Valley. What followed was what one biographer called a darkening of the Stegnerian persona. As Jackson Benson reports in his book *Down by the Lemonade Springs*, Silicon Valley was once the Santa Clara Valley, a delightful region of orchards as well as some vineyards and truck farms. On a sunny day, one could see from high in the green foothills above where Stegner had built his home, over a valley filled with trees to the glittering waters of San Francisco Bay just beyond. Now the air is dense with smog, the roads are choked with traffic, and the farms are covered over by houses and industrial parks. Despite efforts to save it, the bay is badly polluted, a brown mess.

Jackson Benson reports that when the Stegners first built their house, they could look out in the other direction, across the hills behind them, and not see a single light flickering in the darkness. In the years just before Stegner died, the area around his modest ranch-style house became dotted with obscene "castles." Suddenly, over just a few years, the Stegners found themselves surrounded by huge mansions on mini-ranch-sized acreage, mansions usually inhabited by one or two people or owned by absentee Asian entrepreneurs. That people would carve up his beloved foothills as an investment, not even bothering to live there, disturbed Stegner immensely.

In talking about the new West, Stegner claimed there was a sense – to use Gertrude Stein's famous phrase about Oakland – that there was no longer any "there" there: no connection with history, no sense of connection with one's neighbours or sense of community, no feeling of connection with the land or reverence for the natural. In all this, Stegner saw the erosion of the fundamental and founding values of the West. Stegner felt that whatever remained of the uniqueness of Western identity had been subsumed by mass culture. Modern Western individualism was now expressed almost solely through unrestrained corporatism. Whatever he had valued most in the West at one time was now irretrievably gone and could only be recovered in history and nostalgia.

In the face of radical change, Stegner began to feel less certain about the West's chances of creating "a society to match the scenery." Although he had once written, memorably, that the West was "hope's native home," he now admitted that he was not really hopeful about the West's future. Stegner declared that the West was no more the Eden he once thought it was than the Garden of the World that the boosters and engineers tried to make it; and that neither nostalgia nor boosterism could any longer make a case for it as the geography of hope. After *Crossing to Safety*, Stegner made it clear that he no longer held the West to be a geography of hope but a geography of despair. Stegner died from injuries suffered in a car accident in Santa Fe, New Mexico, on March 28, 1993. His ashes were spread, not in the West, but in Vermont.

So, what can we learn from Wallace Stegner about *our* West, which is to say the mountain West in Canada?

For the moment, at least, our West is different from *their* West. But it is changing. Where I live in Canmore people often stay only briefly and then move on. I learned, however, to made it a habit to reserve judgment. Though it happens far less often now that Canmore has become such an expensive place to live, many returned two or three years later to stand sheepishly at my door, and inevitably their story is always the same. They were in some distant mountain range, the Alps, the Andes or perhaps the Himalayas, and they became un-expectedly aware of a sight, a sound or a smell that reminded them of here. The geography of the Rockies had finally captured them, and they had come home. The mountains here have not lost any of their power; what has changed is what it costs to live among them. And the other mountains that beckon have begun to face the same problem.

For the moment, at least, it appears we still have room to move in creating the West we want. If we are able to create a society that matches the setting in which we live, then what we've saved may very well save us. But if Wallace Stegner teaches us anything, it is this: we had better get moving while that room still exists.

Standing History on Its Head

While readers of a book like this will feel a certain grounding in where they live, I am sure you agree that sense of place in our society is not what it used to be. Because of increased mobility, real grounding in place is vanishing from our experience.

As Jack Turner observed in his book *The Abstract Wild*, the antagonists against whom we fight to preserve a lasting, meaningful connection with place are not the usual suspects – cheap global travel, outside developers and real estate speculators, greedy tourism operators, mining and logging companies or any of a dozen other species that oppose the spirit of the wilderness ideal. They may be the principal, immediate problem, but the real problem goes much deeper.

Our greatest enemy with respect to sense of place are abstractions that render even the idea of landscape an abstraction. These include our diminished personal experience of nature; the concomitant devaluation of that experience; and the attendant rise in mediated experience.

Our deepest awareness of where we live is also undermined by our preference for artifice, copy, simulation and surrogate; our attraction to the engineered and managed instead of the natural; and our increasing dependence on experts to control and manipulate a natural world we no longer know.

Our deepest appreciation of where we live is also undermined by our addiction to economics, recreation and amusement at the expense of deeper experiences and values; the increasingly global homogeneity that flattens not only biodiversity but cultural and linguistic diversity; and our increasing ignorance of what we have lost in sacrificing our several-million-year-old intimacy with the natural world.

Perhaps there is an opportunity in what we are going through now to remind ourselves and one another that if we stop stalking it, the world will come to us. What is required of us is that we dig in, become local by choice and allow the spirits of place to speak their names through us. One place to start is with history.

Real places don't just come into existence by accident. We create them. And in this, history matters, for it is the foundation of our identity.

While Indigenous identity is grounded in having occupied the mountain West since time immemorial, settler identity has its roots in the 19th century. The history of the mountains in which I live is still dominated by the age of the railway, an age when men were men and the rest of the animate world was nervous – or should have been. Talk about a male-dominated world! It was a century of men – men translating vision and commitment into meaningful action. Men making their power work for them, in industry, culture and nature. It was an age, so we have been told, of nation building.

This history, of course, was largely constructed by the public relations department of the Canadian Pacific Railway as a means of romanticizing its attractions in the mountain

West. As Indigenous Peoples will explain, the real history – the history we don't like to talk about – is one of colonialism, broken treaties, land theft, racism and social injustice that we have only begun to address at last through a national commitment to truth and ultimate reconciliation. But there are parts of that romantic history that are worth salvaging.

As a lifelong student of natural and human history, I do not think it unreasonable to make bold new claims about the history of Canada's mountain West. I believe we have a false sense of history, not just in the Rockies but in the Purcells, Selkirks, Monashees and Cascades. I believe we have derived the wrong lessons from the past and that it is time to stand Western Canadian history on its head.

My first new claim is that we have got our history backward. Our greatest cultural achievement in the mountain region of Western Canada is not what we think it is. It is not what we have developed in terms of infrastructure, industry, commerce or human settlement and population growth that has in the end defined us. While we've always marked development as central to our history as we have traditionally defined it, the reality is that railways, highways, towns and cities only partly define our deeper identity.

My second claim is that the products of the human desire to modify and urbanize the places in which we live will not define our identity in the future in the same ways that they will in so many other places in Canada.

The mountain West is different from the rest of the country – and from most of the rest of the continent – in that it is not what we've constructed out of the landscape that most deeply and enduringly defines us as a people. It is not what we've built that truly makes us unique as a culture, but what we've saved.

In the midst of fragmenting and developing the mountain West, we recognized there were qualities of place here that meant something more to us than immediate wealth. Slowly and haltingly we undertook steps that would allow elements of the West we cherished to be preserved and protected. After discovering what we had, we began to put what we had started to destroy back together again in a semblance of its original pristine form.

Instead of simply overwhelming place and developing it into something it wasn't before, locals accommodated the landscape and allowed it in part to define local character and culture. What makes the foundation of culture in the mountain West unique is the extent to which locals have historically cared about the landscapes upon which they live and the degree of ritual and actual sacrifice they are prepared to undertake to ensure that qualities of place endure from one generation to the next.

Once the pieces were saved, it gradually occurred to us that their collective value was far more than the sum of their parts. It took nearly a century for the value of what we had done to soak in.

In 1984 the four mountain national parks, Banff, Jasper, Kootenay and Yoho, were, based on the remarkable geological features they protected, together granted UNESCO World Heritage Site designation.

But that was only a prelude to further designations that created one of the most remarkable and significant large-scale ecological and cultural reserves in the world.

Once again it took time to fully recognize what we have. It has taken more than 20 years to realize that what we had created is one of the greatest collective expressions of the will to protect national heritage the world has ever witnessed.

Each of these acts of creation was undertaken because locals wanted something more than a West overwhelmed by established forms of development. No one attempted to anticipate or could have imagined at the time how

remarkably important the creation of each element in this network would ultimately become.

In my mind, this act of gradual affirma-
tion of our identity as a people is the greatest
public policy achievement in the history of the
Canadian West and should be celebrated as
such.

What We Saved Could Now Save Us

Another bold assertion I would like to make
with respect to our history and identity is that
in protecting the spine of the Rocky Mountains
we have preserved ecological functions that
will be of inestimable value in the future.

Not only have we slowed the process of
ecosystem diminishment and species loss that
have so affected our continent since the end of
the last Ice Age, we have kept alive an ecological thermostat that may well be an important
defence against future human use and climate

change impacts in the Canadian West. What we saved might now save us.

It is this way of thinking, this very process of establishing, maintaining and strengthening our identity, however, that is currently under threat. If we are going to save what has saved us, we need to wake up now. Our very greatest achievements are under threat. Our very history and our identity are under siege.

True sustainability may be beyond our grasp if we don't do the right thing now. Many believe that, if only out of sheer necessity, we will adapt and become more resilient as a society. But we can and need to do more. We keep talking about adaptation in service of resilience; but resilience implies protecting what we have now. We need to be *pre-silient*; we need to protect what we have, certainly, but more than that we need to adapt now for what is to come. And what is coming is a storm.

The Overstory

The Coming Storm

Today, only 1 per cent of the terrestrial Earth is considered uninhabitable. It is projected that climate heating will increase that number to 20 per cent in the future. The alarms went off years ago, but so far we have ignored them.

Because of climate warming impacts, the habitable zone in the United States is already shrinking northward toward Canada. Much of south Florida, the Carolinas, the American West and Southwest are projected to soon be barely habitable. Where will these people go? They will go uphill and to higher latitudes for cooler temperatures to avoid heat and wildfire;

inland away from ever more violent hurricanes and rapid coastal sea level rise; and they will gravitate toward places with reliable water security. Sound like any place you might know?

This northward movement is already occurring globally. If you don't think this will affect where you live, think again. Many in the advance wave have money, and nothing will stop them. And they are only the first wave. Whether you like it or not, the people who want what we have are coming. Get ready.

If our mountain communities have no idea of how to counter dispossession now, how will they retain their character and authenticity when under siege? Hard to say. It isn't even on our radar yet.

Then there is the global circumstance. The UN predicts 200 million involuntary human migrants by 2050. If 2020 was any indication, we are in for a perfect storm. If we in the mountain West want to get ahead of that storm, the first thing we ought to do is recognize it is coming and prepare for it.

So how do we prepare? We can begin by using our past and the West we have created to help define the West we want in the future. We have done it once and we can do it again.

The coming decade will be a crucial breakdown or breakthrough period in the history of humanity. This decade will certainly be a turning point in how we choose to live in the West.

We are running out of time to reconsider what kind of West we want: not just the economic, cultural or virtual landscape we want to create, but the physical West that will provide our inspiration and our solace and shape our deepest identity as a people sharing an astonishing landscape. It can't just be about money. There is no time for delay. Even before COVID, we knew we needed to get moving if we wanted to create a culture commensurate with place. COVID only put into bold relief the need to do so.

The pandemic shook us awake. We were forced to pause and take stock of ourselves. Who are we? Who do we want to be?

There is an old saying that if you can't fish, then spend the time mending your nets. For me, that means reaffirming my connection to place.

It has been an interesting journey. Love of these mountains has given my life meaning, purpose and direction. Nothing will erode my deep, abiding and hard-won sense of place. I must admit, however, that there were periods – sometimes long periods – when my faith in place has been severely tested. For many years now I have heard the word *solastalgia* mentioned in circles concerned about the integrity of unique geo-cultural regions like the Canadian Rockies. Solastalgia, I am told, is the condition of being homesick in a home place that has been degraded or destroyed.

At first, I rather dismissed solastalgia as just one more academic term brought into existence to describe yet another debilitating pseudo-psychological malady for which you could get a doctor's note that would get you six months of paid stress leave if you worked for the right government agency. I don't dismiss it now. The pandemic has put a lot of things into bold relief.

Since I moved here the entire character of the town has changed. Over time, the population of Calgary grew so much that Canmore essentially became a trendy neighbourhood and Banff little more than an upscale city park. Soon there were more people coming here during midwinter than we saw on the busiest summer days in 1970.

For the past 20 years, I now acknowledge, I really did grow more and more homesick for what we had lost, for all that has been degraded by greed, certainly, but also unwittingly by people who ruin what they are coming for by virtue of their sheer numbers. I didn't leave this place. I felt that it left me. But then, just as I wondered when the entire lattice of the relentless desire for more and more and more would collapse, along came the pandemic, which in a few weeks turned the clock back 50 years.

Though we may not be able to use this potentially transformational moment to halt and reverse the degradation and destruction of elements of place that give so much meaning and value to where and how we live in these mountains, at least we may be able to slow it down. The Great Pause gives us an opportunity not just to mend our nets, but to rethink what we are fishing for and, ultimately, to examine if it is even fishing that we want to be doing in the future.

I used this Precious Pause to reimagine where and how I live. And it's working. The slowing down has the solastalgia on the run. Everyday miracles have become apparent again. The foxes I've been hearing for years are slowly making their way into the front ranges, we can now actually see.

I'm catching up on reading and perhaps more importantly finding deeper meaning in what I have already read but didn't have enough time to process completely enough to stitch into my knowing and being.

I have, for example, been pushing from the top down to find ways of finally implementing the United Nations 2030 *Transforming Our World* global sustainable development goals at national, subnational and municipal levels in this and other countries. It has been an uphill slog. But now, because of the Great Pause, American writer Wendell Berry has been able to help me understand why it has been so difficult. In an essay he published in 1989 titled "The Futility of Global Thinking," Berry asserted that "no place on earth can be completely healthy until all places are.... The question that must be addressed is not how to care for the planet, but how to care for each of the planet's millions of human and natural neighborhoods...which is in some precious way different from all the others." I should point out that Berry wrote that 33 years ago.

Place and placelessness. Here the erosion of place has been sponsored primarily by transplanted opportunists pursuing lifestyle fantasies, as well as the usual corporate exploiters ever more hungry for greater profits. As Wendell Berry puts it, these people have no local allegiances; if they had a local point of view it would be unconscionable to desecrate, endanger or destroy a *place*. (His emphasis, not mine.)

As I have clearly witnessed here, it is not always those who have lived here the longest but those who are most deeply rooted in place who are most likely to fight the hardest for the qualities of the place because they know and can stand up for that which makes their place desirable to live in and visit. While such resistance is not understood in many circumstances and is often simply dismissed as an unwillingness to accept change, what is often missed is that these people are fighting *for* a way of life, not *against* one. And that, I see now, is the way sustainability has to be seen here and in all of the millions of unique human and natural neighbourhoods on the planet.

By far the greatest benefit of being forced to pause in my life now is that it is allowing me to look back on my experience here with greater cumulative understanding and appreciation, which has led to a deeper sense of place than I have ever possessed before. Working with youth on water and water-related climate matters has given me greater hope for the future than I have possessed since I arrived here as a young man. As I shall later report, the enthusiasm, intelligence, courage and honesty of a group of 12- to 19-year-olds I have been working with have renewed my faith in the world, and that has restored my idealism and sense of wonder. I am seeing the world afresh. I have reawakened to its wonders.

If you were in the high-risk cohort to die if you contracted the virus, you were advised not to go far, if you went anywhere at all. That meant you had to get the most out of the nature immediately around you. Fortunately, the back deck of our house looks out on prime montane forest.

I have for years looked forward to the day when I could at last sit back and rejoice in the spectacular views living here affords. That time has come.

I have time to observe and listen to the trees. I watch a pair of robins as they construct a nest in a tall white spruce. A raven silently glides over the trees, no doubt noting the location of the nest building. In the spirit of animated taxonomy I named that raven CORVID-19.

After hurriedly reading it when it was published, I have returned to *The Hidden Life of Trees* by Peter Wohlleben. I recognized then that there were important new research outcomes that I'd hoped to one day have time to assimilate into my world view. Over the last ten years in particular I have been coming increasingly to the realization that the Earth is far more sentient than we know or can know. Wohlleben's book supports that supposition.

I have to admit that at first some of what Wohlleben was putting forward sounded like a lot of woo-woo, and I also submit that I have yet to find much in the scientific literature to support many of his claims. But that the renowned Australian Earth scientist Tim Flannery endorsed the book was all the encouragement I needed. I was hoping that the woo-woo would turn into woo-hoo!

In his excellent introduction to *The Hidden Life of Trees*, Flannery observes that one of the reasons many of us fail to understand and fully appreciate trees is that they live on different time scales than we do.

He notes that an ancient spruce in Sweden has been determined to be 9,500 years old, which means it has lived 115 times longer than the average human lifetime. For creatures that can live that long, taking a couple of years' time out to allow a pandemic to pass is barely a slight bend of a bough in a light May breeze.

Eternity as we perceive it is that which might move us during a visit to a cathedral. The eternity trees bespeak is ageless beyond what we know from our experience, beyond what we can conceive.

As Flannery points out, creatures with as much time on their hands as trees can afford to function at a more leisurely pace. And they do. Electrical impulses that pass through their roots, for example – and electrical impulses apparently do spark through their roots – move at a rate of roughly 0.85 cm per second. Why, Flannery then asks, do trees pass electrical impulses through their tissues at all? The answer, astonishingly, is that trees need to communicate with one another and electrical impulses are one way of doing so.

Trees also, we are now told, possess senses of smell and taste. This, as Flannery puts it, suggests that life in the slow lane is a lot more interesting than we thought. I hope this is a discovery a lot of us make as we move through this uncertain time.

The most astonishing thing about trees, Flannery continues, is how social they are. Evidence suggests the trees even go so far as to care for one another, sometimes to the point of trees nourishing a stump of a tree for centuries after it was cut down by feeding it sugars and nutrients to keep it alive.

It would almost seem as if the stumps are the parents of the trees and forests where this happens.

Flannery goes on to explain that the tree's most effective way of socializing is through social media – a "World Wood Web," as Wohlleben calls it.

This amazing web is composed of soil fungi that connect trees by way of a complex but intimate subsurface network of information and goods sharing that we are only beginning to understand. The reason trees share information and even food is that they need each other. Forests are living things in themselves and, like us, create the microclimates most suitable for the forest's existence and perpetuation. In other words, the oldest living things on the terrestrial Earth are social systems. Individuals take care of one another. It's not surprising, then, that, just as in human societies, isolated trees have far shorter lives than those living close to others in a forest.

Perhaps the saddest plants of all, Flannery maintains, are those enslaved in agricultural systems. Citing Wohlleben, Flannery notes that these plants have essentially lost the ability to communicate. The slaves of the plant world, agricultural crops have all the appearance of being struck deaf and dumb.

Wohlleben offers that perhaps farmers could learn from forests and breed a little wildness back into our wheat and our potatoes so they will be more talkative in the future.

And so, I begin again with this book, which I will take the time to thoughtfully and with purpose reread among the slow talking, electrically charged and social media–savvy trees in the very much sentient forest in my own backyard.

I suspect, now that I have been told that trees experience pain and possess memories and that tree parents live together with their children, that I will never look again at these trees in the backyard in the same way. They have much to teach me and I committed to spending the summer of the Great Pause learning to hear them and perhaps coming to understand all that we commonly smell and taste and ultimately share on this most astounding and wondrous Earth.

I believed we would get through this pandemic if we paid attention and persisted in making this great and precious pause into a transformational moment – an actual global reset – we could make this a better world. But to achieve that vision we have to act upon the realization that there's never been a time in our lives when accurate intellectual, emotional, joyful and spiritually moving communication will matter more.

It's at times like this that important words fall into disuse, overwhelmed by louder, more oft-repeated others. It's at times like this that words fall through the cracks. The problem here is that once words disappear, the things and ideas those words represent can disappear. Words and what they mean can lose force. In terms of sense of place, we can't let that happen.

Stewards and spokespersons for what is important about where and how we live in the mountain West need now to reaffirm and repeat again and again the words and celebrate the ideas and experiences that shape our identity and define who we are, and who we want to be, in this most unique and intact of all the world's human and natural neighbourhoods.

COVID Comes Knocking

Letter to the Editor
Making Masks Mandatory
R.W. Sandford

I wear a mask to protect you; will you not wear a mask to protect me? No! It offends you to have to wear a mask during a global public health emergency!

I get it. I can see how you feel that way. The pandemic is inconvenient. It seems to have stalled everything, and that is frustrating. It is easy to think that because of COVID, nothing is happening. But as we enter into the cold and the darkness, maybe it's time to think in broader terms. While it may not appear so at the moment, something *is* happening. Something big. Forget all the other threats humanity faces for the moment; forget all that is backing up behind the COVID dam. The virus isn't just killing us and pushing our health systems past their limits, it is killing our economies and damaging our political structures and institutions. Unchecked, one way or another the virus could take us out, and not just some of us, but enough of us to make a difference to the future.

Care to talk about a transformational moment in the course of human history? We are living in one. And how are we handling it? "Don't tell me I have to wear a mask. You are impinging on my individual rights, my freedoms." Nice to have rights; but rights come with responsibilities. If we don't handle this pandemic right a lot more of us are going to die. Look around you. Take note of who your friends are and which of your family members you are among. Imagine next what it would be like to lose half of them. Now, take a break from your selfish protest against wearing a mask and contemplate which of your family and friends you would least like to infect; name the ones you would spare and which you would condemn to death.

I asked a judge about whether or not killing someone without malice or aforethought or in circumstances that did not amount to murder was a crime. "Yes," the judge said, "it's called manslaughter."

When you walk into a shop or a restaurant without wearing a mask and belligerently proclaim, "I am OK!" should I believe you? Or should I fear and perhaps despise you because I know that you could, through your arrogance, ignorance and wilful blindness, actually kill me?

Parable of the Robin

As I maintained throughout the months of pandemic house arrest, one does not need to aggressively seek or go afar to find ecological connection. All you need to do is find some backyard from which you can observe what is happening in and beneath the trees and, if you are patient, ecological connection will come to you. Many of us were fortunate enough to have such backyards. That was reaffirmed in the early summer of the first COVID year, when my wife Vi entered the living room from the back deck to announce that hope incarnate had appeared in our backyard in the form of a robin nesting upon a light fixture under the eaves of our house.

After all the books I have read (and written) about hope; all the deep and solemn conversations about hope and its meaning; all the anguished and heartfelt emails and well-meaning dispatches; all the hand-wringing about our future; all the emotional ups-and-downs since the pandemic began; it all suddenly seemed less relevant when my wife came in from the back deck and offered, in a few sentences, a living parable of a robin. "Here is what is going on in the backyard," she said. "There is a female robin out there sitting patiently and resolutely on her blue eggs in a nest under the eaves with no certainty that the eggs will even hatch and even less certainty that the young will live to fledge. That," she said, "is all you need to know about hope. You are looking for hope, there it is."

It took a few moments for that statement to crystallize. Then it struck me that her simple observation at once affirmed and yet transcended everything I have ever read or said or written to inspire confidence in our collective ability to create the world we want. While the challenge of societal transformation is complex, the notion of hope is not.

My wife's simple parable gives me more hope than all I have read and said and done, certainly since the pandemic began, but also in the years leading up to it during which I feared for the future. It is a parable that reveals not just the preciousness but the sacredness of all life. It reminds us that we are not the only ones on this planet in possession of, and in need of, hope. It also puts into relief the obvious fact that by way of our self-centredness and thoughtlessness as a species we are not only robbing other sentient beings and the rest of the world of hope, we are threatening their very existence and in so doing undermining and threatening our own.

That tiny ball of hollow bones wrapped in fuzz and feathers managed to lay four eggs. Hope to the 4th power. All four of those eggs hatched; hope to the 16th power. That the four hatchlings then successfully fledged from the same nest is an expression of infinite, unconditional hope affirmed. The pulse of hope is life. In our backyard, the agency of that hope was an emaciated, exhausted but still singing mother robin.

But the parable doesn't end there. Most know what a robin is, but do they know what it means to *be* a robin? To be a robin is to embody hope. The average American robin weighs only 77 grams, or about 2¾ ounces. That is how much hope can be packed into even the smallest and lightest forms of life. How much hope can we pack into our lives? Surely as much as a robin.

Hope, for the moment, remains firmly established as a principal element of backyard ecological diplomacy. The expanded geopolitics of our backyard remain stable. If one sits long enough and watches, it is possible to feel radical empathy not just toward other people but toward all life. If you can feel such empathy in your backyard, it should be possible to carry that empathy with you wherever you go. So singeth the robin.

Drinking Beer with Albert Camus on Canada Day
Thursday, July 1, 2021

Today is the day that the Government of Alberta officially declared that the province could "open up again," and that people no longer need concern themselves with social distancing or wearing a mask if they did not want to. In other words, they have essentially declared the pandemic over. Since the virus and its mob of unruly variants were not consulted on the matter, only time will tell if that is really true. It is a good juncture, however, to reflect on what we've experienced since the first lockdown in March of last year, and today – Canada Day – the day Alberta declared that the pandemic was at last under control. One way of doing that is to compare our experiences with those of others who have found themselves isolated in quarantine in similar epidemic circumstances. And that is why I invited the ghost of Albert Camus along for a drink on the deck of the Rose and Crown Pub.

It is interesting that while I read Albert Camus and the French writers of that era extensively in my 20s and early 30s, I never read Camus's *The Plague*. It is as if I had to wait until this pandemic to read it. It is important also to note that the plague about which Camus writes was not a virus like COVID-19, but the gram-negative bacterium *Yersina pestis*, which throughout human history has caused many outbreaks of the bubonic plague. While the novel is about an outbreak of bubonic plague in Algeria in the 1940s, which did occur, most of the plot and the medical science and history upon which the plot turns come from Camus's obviously very thorough research into what happened in Algeria's second largest city, Oran, during a brutal cholera outbreak that wiped out a large part of the population in 1849. Cholera has long been a scourge in the region. Over a period of only 75 years, 49 cholera and bubonic plague outbreaks resulted in 7,612 cases in 30 locations in the Arab Maghreb (Mauritania, Morocco, Algeria, Tunisia, Libya and Egypt). By the time Camus wrote *The Plague*, both cholera and the plague still lingered throughout North Africa. Perhaps more than any other writer, Camus captured what that meant to the people and the communities that fell under threat and the horror many suffered or to which all were exposed over the long months of quarantine and isolation.

I did not get around to reading *The Plague* until six months into our pandemic. At that time, August 2020, there was no end in sight. Camus describes in his novel the entire process of surviving a full outbreak of bubonic plague in a port city. We follow the impacts and consequences for local people and the community from the beginning to the end of the scourge. What astonished me about the novel was that instead of being published in French in 1947, it could just as easily have been published last Tuesday. In instance after instance, description after description, I had to put the book down and remind myself that he was describing a fictional plague in the 1940s and not what I was personally experiencing in a COVID-19 pandemic in 2020.

As we were all in the early stages of the pandemic then, I thought it might be instructive to return to Camus's fictional account to see if we could learn from similarities between our two circumstances, now that at least some among us believe that this pandemic is coming at last to an end, at least here in Alberta. And in retrospect there are a great many similarities, which I will present in the order in which they appear in the book.

When it first became clear that they were indeed facing a plague and that they would have to take drastic measures to confine it to the town, the authorities in Camus's narrative were reluctant to face the facts and were quite prepared to say it wasn't the plague. It quickly became apparent, however, that it didn't really matter whether you called it a plague or some other fever, the important thing was to prevent its killing off half the population of the town. But even when it became evident that it would be necessary to apply the rigorous prophylactic measures laid down in the health code, some of the authorities maintained that there was no absolute certainty that this was, in fact, the plague and that hasty action should be avoided. "Wait and see" was their approach.

At first the measures the authorities put in place were far from draconian, and one had the feeling that many concessions had been made to a desire not to inconvenience or alarm the public.

It soon became apparent what they faced was a full-blown plague and that the only hope was that the outbreak would die a natural death, as it certainly wouldn't be arrested by the measures the authorities had so far devised. Vaccines were also a possibility, but so far none existed and the possibility of creating them was months, if not years, away. Quarantine was the only viable option. A state of plague was proclaimed.

The proclamation of the lockdown was met with fierce resistance from those who did not want to interrupt commerce or close the city's thriving port (read "airport" here).

One of the most striking consequences of the lockdown was the sudden deprivation befalling people who were completely unprepared for it.

The normal feelings of separation from those one loved suddenly became a feeling all shared alike and – together with fear – the greatest affliction of a long period of enforced self-isolation ahead.

The restrictions were meant to apply to all, and for a time words like "special arrangements," "privilege" and "priority" lost their meaning and later came to be despised as the wealthy tried to reinvigorate them.

The drastic deprivation and total uncertainty with respect to the future had taken all unawares. The sensation of a void within grew and never left, but instead hardened into an irrational longing to hearken back to the past or else speed up the march of time. Six months into the lockdown it became clear that the disease that had already pinned everyone down for half a year could easily last much longer, perhaps a year or even more. Drained of the past, impatient of the present and cheated of the future, many began to feel imprisoned. Some wearied of what had become almost unbearable leisure and were only able to hold themselves together with dreams of exotic future travel. Others forced themselves not to think about the problematic day of escape from the pandemic and ceased looking to the future, preferring, so to speak, to keep their eyes focused on the ground at their feet. This, however, was ill-rewarded, for in taking a middle course in managing their isolation, they drifted through life rather than lived, and they became the prey, as Camus put it, "of aimless days and sterile memories like wandering shadows that could have acquired substance only by consenting to root themselves in the solid earth of their distress."

The unmerited distress imposed on those who in no way felt they deserved to be visited by such a foreign pestilence incited some to create their own suffering and thus to accept frustration as a natural state. This was one of the ways the pestilence had of diverting attention and confounding issues related to compliance with health measures.

Despite heroic efforts to keep it fully alive, commerce too died of the plague. The first reaction to this was to abuse the authorities. It was not until the death rate continued to rise that people began to fully see the truth of the situation and ceased persisting in the idea that what was happening was a sort of accident, disagreeable certainly, but of a temporary order.

People started drinking heavily, claiming alcohol to be a safeguard against infection.

Pressure on the authorities continued under the argument that scientific evidence was an abstraction, and that matters of the heart were more compelling in terms of separation from loved ones. More than 500 deaths a week, however, proved to be no minor abstraction, nor was the need to separate the sick from their families an abstraction. But while some saw abstractions and fought the science, others saw truth. Yes, an element of abstraction, of a divorce from reality, entered into such calamities. Still, when abstraction sets to killing you, you can't ignore it.

The truth was that nothing is less sensational than a pestilence, and by reason of their very duration, great misfortunes are monotonous. In the memories of those who lived through them, the grim days of pandemic did not stand out like vivid flames, ravenous and inextinguishable, but rather like the slow, deliberate progress of some monstrous thing crushing out all upon its path.

The plague had its own genius. It was as if it knew exactly what it was doing. Infections killed all colours and classes indiscriminately and vetoed pleasures.

The daily reports of the number of infections and deaths soon became sterile statistics. It was as if the authorities in the media were reporting box scores in a World Series of infection and death.

Then gradually there came a general loss of the capacity for exalted emotion. Emotions became trite and monotonous. "It is high time it stopped," people would say, because in a time of calamity the obvious thing is to desire its end, but in making these remarks there was none of the passionate yearning or fierce resentment of the early phase of the lockdown. The confusion and revolt against the idea of being locked down and out that characterized the first weeks had been replaced by a vast despondency, not to be taken as resignation, though it was nonetheless a sort of passive acquiescence, that for some gave way to the gnawing, insatiable hunger of separation.

It wasn't long before, if you listened for it, you could hear the sound of a huge concourse of people marking time.

The crisis, obviously, put a huge strain on doctors and the health care system as a whole. Doctors and those assisting them became too exhausted to keep to strict safeguards for their own protection. Some doctors died and more lost members of their families. Camus vividly details horrifying death scenes, scenes similar to those that have created so much grief worldwide as a consequence of the COVID-19 pandemic.

Over time, prices rose and there was profligate spending. While necessities were sometimes in short supply, never had so much been spent on superfluities. All the recreations of leisure, due in part to unemployment, multiplied a hundredfold.

Amazingly, in both instances, health authorities became obsessed with "flattening the curve." The fact that the graph representing the number of cases, after its long rising, flattened out was taken to mean that the disease has reached its high-water mark, and that thereafter it would ebb. But in both cases, as the initial curve flattened, the disease pathogens took on new forms. In Camus's account, the bubonic plague was replaced by a more lethal pneumonic plague. In 2021, COVID-19 evolved into ever more contagious variants of the virus. In both instances social distancing and wearing a mask was deemed to be critical to halt the spread of the disease.

As the months passed, the lockdown circumstances put into ever more glaring relief the inequalities that existed between the haves and the poor. Many came to despise the public health measures imposed upon them, the vilest of them being those that demanded quarantine. Breaches of peace, demonstrations against lockdown measures and even minor riots became more frequent. Those who protested against and refused to follow public health measures never grasped the fact that in resisting these measures they were extending the very lockdown measures they professed to hate, while at the same time endangering their own lives and the lives of all around them.

For Camus, the plague was a metaphor for a larger plague we all carried within us which infects our entire society. (In evaluating this metaphor we must remember that the period in which Camus wrote his book was a turbulent time of war and death.) As time went on, it occurred to Camus, such was the logic of the time that even those who were better than the rest could not keep themselves from killing or letting others kill. Such were the circumstances of the time that it was impossible to lift a finger without the risk of bringing death to someone or something. Because of this, one had to do what one could to cease being plague stricken, for that was the only way one could hope for some peace, and, failing that, a decent death. The only way we can bring relief to our society, he wrote, if not to save it, was to do the least harm possible and even, sometimes a little good. One could choose not to join up with the pestilences, but it was wearying to refuse to do so. That's why, even though everyone was more or less sick of the plague, even those who wanted to get the plague out of their systems felt such frustration and desperation. All had the plague within them; no one on Earth is free from it. For that reason, all of us must keep endless watch on ourselves lest we infect others. What is natural is the microbe, the virus. All the rest, health, integrity, purity – our very sustainability – is the product of human will. Everything good and enduring about our lives and our world is a product of a vigilance that must never fail.

Only when it began to weaken did people start talking of a new order of life they would settle into after the plague. The decline of the disease, however, occurred haltingly. Only slowly did the treatments the medical profession employed without definite results become uniformly efficacious. It was as if the disease had been hounded down and cornered. It was, however, doubtful whether this could be called a victory. It was as if the epidemic had called a retreat after reaching all of its objectives; it had, so to speak, achieved its purpose. It could be said that once the stirring of hope became possible, the dominion of the infection was ended, which had deeper repercussions, including an unaccountable drop in prices.

A tentative announcement that the plague was at its end came with a stern warning that there were no assurances. The plague, or another like it, could return at any time. The only ones who did not celebrate were those still in mourning and those whose family members were sick or in quarantine. But even then, people continued to be diagnosed with having the original infection as well as the new variant. The disease never did confess defeat.

And though there may have been an armistice of sorts, the war went on in the hearts and memories of those who lost loved ones. Others, who were not ready for the joy after all those days and weeks of life lost, could never again regain happiness. For them the time of forgetting would never come.

The most pronounced differences between Camus's account of the plague in North Africa set in the 1940s and COVID-19 now reside in the fact that COVID was a global pandemic, not a local epidemic, and that in our time we were able to create and mobilize vaccines to fight the virus and its evolving variants. Neither Camus's nor ours is an account of victory, but in both we arrive at the realization that there is one thing we can always yearn for and sometimes attain, and that is human love. A final lesson we might learn from Camus's plague and our pandemic is that there is more in humanity to admire than to despise; and that all of this would have to be done again, in our never-ending fight against pathogens within, and the Anthropocene we have created for ourselves that plagues us from without. Neither has gone away.

No one wanted to hear it on Canada Day, the day of the reopening; but both will be back.

Meanwhile, as COVID shuffled grumbling off into the wings, climate heating was taking the main stage at Canada Day celebrations.

Meet the COVID-Climate Tag Team

It wasn't long into the pandemic that we were reminded once again that one crisis doesn't simply end with the arrival of another. While we seemed to be on top of the pandemic by June of 2021, we suddenly realized that COVID and climate disruption actually *were* a tag team.

While COVID took a bit of a rest to brew up more infectious variants, and anti-vaxxers queued up in parades to expose themselves to them, the pandemic tagged climate heating, and the latter thundered into the ring stronger than ever.

COVID put into relief the gap between the rich and the poor; climate change has exposed the further and growing gap between the expectations of the young and the old.

You didn't need to be a scientist to see this. Where I live, all you had to do was look out the window. What happened in British Columbia and throughout the Canadian West during the summer and in the fall of 2021, and what continues to happen now, should be regarded as a 9/11-like event that wakes us all up to the climate emergency we knew was coming.

We have known for a long time that this day would eventually arrive if we continued to ignore the warnings and the evidence of the risks we were taking by not acting on the climate threat. But we did not expect that climate change impacts that were projected to appear by mid-century would arrive 20 to 30 years early. The West got slammed. We are the epicentre of the epicentre of global change, the same change that is coming soon to a theatre near you, no matter where you live.

Remember that this is Canada. You know, the land of ice and snow. Under the June heat dome 700 people died of heat stress in the Greater Vancouver area alone. By only a few days into July, 300 all-time-high temperature records had already been broken in British Columbia, 125 more in Alberta. These records were not just broken; they were being shattered day after day, ultimately by as much as 5 to 8°C.

By Canada Day, four million British Columbians and ten million people in Western Canada alone had been exposed to a major unprecedented weather event.

Then, suddenly, temperatures reached 49.6°C in Lytton, BC, which, it has been noted, is higher than the record high temperature in Las Vegas, Nevada. Lytton broke the previous high temperature record for Canada, set on the prairies in 1934, by almost 5°C. I don't need to tell you that at 50°C almost everything becomes more combustible. The fire that destroyed Lytton shocked climate scientists around the world.

But what we faced at that time was not over. In June alone there were 5,770 high temperatures records broken in North America, most of them in the last few days of the month. Drought spread from Vancouver Island to Quebec. In many places, crops started to fail. There were also other significant losses that went largely unnoticed.

Research conducted by the Western Canadian Cryospheric Network has demonstrated that we lost some 300 glaciers in the mountain national parks region of the Rockies alone in the 85 years between 1920 and 2005. Melted glacial ice makes more liquid water available to an already energized water cycle. This loss of glaciers was expected to continue, with over 90 per cent of the ice that exists in the interior ranges of Canada's western mountains expected to be gone perhaps by the end of this century but not before. Or so we thought.

The Peyto Glacier is at the headwaters of the North Saskatchewan River system, one of the most important rivers of the West, so what happens here matters.

Over the last 25 years, the Peyto Glacier has receded on average 25 metres a year. In 2021 the Peyto receded 200 metres, eight times the average loss over the last quarter-century. It has also down-wasted by 15 metres in only two years. This rate of glacial loss is unprecedented in the more than a century during which the dynamics of this glacier have been scientifically monitored.

At this rate of recession, researchers expect the Peyto Glacier will not exist much beyond this decade and that by the end of the century, only 3 per cent will remain of the Wapta Icefield from which it has flowed since time immemorial.

We have known for years that glacial ice is a symptom of a much larger problem. The same warming that is causing our glaciers to disappear so quickly is reducing snowpack and the duration and extent of snow cover throughout the mountain West. We have discovered that winter snows and mountain snowpacks thermo-regulate the climate and define water security for the entire West. The West will soon be a very different place. Welcome to the future.

So that was here. What about elsewhere? If you want to see what the future looks like for others, look no farther than the American West. The drought that had been gripping the American West had become so deep and persistent, and had put into relief so many compound, cumulative and cascading impacts, that many were calling it "the Everything Disaster."

Then came the autumn of 2021. It is typically coastal regions that are hit first and hardest by the effects of atmospheric rivers and cyclones, but now, because of the warming climate, atmospheric rivers are increasing in intensity to such an extent that they are penetrating more deeply and powerfully inland. Just as we are not ready for prolonged heat domes, summer temperatures of 50°C, and unimagined fire seasons, we, and our built infrastructure, are not ready for this.

The very geography of British Columbia has been altered. If the rest of the country should learn anything from the climate 9/11 that has unfolded there it is that we live in an often haphazardly constructed world only partially adapted to the relatively stable climate regime that has existed in our time. That time is now over.

We have created the potential for a permanently and perpetually perfect storm in terms of the impacts of climate disruption here and everywhere.

We now exist in a climate regime humanity has never experienced before and to which anything less than a well-organized, aggressive and globally coherent response will be fatal to millions.

We waited too long, and now the hour is late. We squandered hope when we had it, and now hope is abandoning us. If we want to bring hope back, and we want to end this perfect storm – and this climate emergency – we have to wake up and act as though our lives and our futures depend upon immediate action. Because they do. The IPCC agreed.

In June of that fateful year, it was clear that the global climate had begun to change; this was further confirmed with the release of the Working Group I IPCC Assessment Review 6. Climate change is clearly an experiment we should not be conducting. Assessment Review 6 reported that climate change is widespread, rapid, intensifying and accelerating. This is for real, and it is for good. And we are the cause. There is nowhere to run, nowhere to hide. No one is safe. The secretary-general of the United Nations declared it Code Red for the planet. You can't state any warning more clearly than that.

Burning Testament

In forcing myself to examine carefully and honestly where I stood now that it was impossible to deny that we face a planetary emergency, it did not take long to realize how much I have over time been gradually paralyzed by growing anxiety, born of helplessness, that I had to fight to avoid debilitating despair.

I was surprised that getting back to the roots of my deepening anxiety demanded I go back ten years to once again face the failures of courage in my life that Terry Tempest Williams challenged me through her writing to examine.

Tempest Williams is right. The onslaught of public relations and aggressive self-interest in our society has made many of us fear and suspect our deepest feelings of connection within us. Over time, we do come to settle for or accept the inevitability of loss of what is at the root of our connection with place. And that, to a very real extent, is what I had allowed to happen to me.

But Terry Tempest Williams would not accept my moral lapse and, worse than that, wouldn't leave me alone. In *When Women Were Birds* she called me out for my loss of moral courage when she wrote, "To be numb to the world is another form of suicide." I realize now that I have trended and continue to trend self-destructively toward that end. My fear of loss had become so great that it literally hurt me to visit the places I so care about. It was as if I was suffering from a form of pre-traumatic stress disorder – if such a condition could be said to exist. It is almost as if my heart is already broken so there is no longer any *point* in risking giving my love away.

Even though I knew it is unproductive to live like this, I had yet to find the strength to stand fully by my principles. Because I knew that if I did I would alienate almost everyone around me, I just pretended to go along, to live with the crassness that is undermining my community, with the destruction of place, with the trashing of our national parks, with the changing of the composition of the Earth's atmosphere and the acidification and deoxygenation of the global ocean. The list of what we accept goes on and on. All I felt I could do was bear witness.

But, no dice, Terry Tempest Williams said. Not good enough.

If you want to live a moral life on a planet in peril, Terry Tempest Williams will tell you that you won't make it if you're incapable of spiritual resistance – "the ability to stand firm at the center of our convictions when everything around us asks us to concede, that our capacity to face the harsh measures of a life comes from the deep quiet of listening to the land, the river, the rocks." It was because I believed in her, and I could no longer bottle up my love for where I lived and confine my rage within, that I wrote *The Weekender Effect*.

And now, like a spirit helper, Terry Tempest Williams returned to help the growing numbers of Westerners who believe in her get through what was till then the worst fire season in history. On September 20, 2020, Terry Tempest Williams shared her *Burning Testament*, a placeholder for all of us in the then burning West. South of us, and across the artificial line that separates our two countries, five million acres of forest had burned so suddenly that, as Tempest Williams put it, it melted the capacity of stunned victims to feel the magnitude of what had happened.

With the fires approaching where she lived, there was little anyone could do but watch and wait. "We are not okay." she reported. "We are anxious. We are scared. There is no place to hide. There is only our love and our grief to hold us in the terror of all we are seeing, sensing and denying. We can't touch the source of our despair because we can't touch each other. And so we retreat inside when everything outside is screaming. We are sitting in rooms watching screens alone, waiting as if this is a pause instead of a place...."

The facts, she testified, did not tell the story of how their hearts were breaking, nor did the photographs of the blackened forests. The news, she reported, failed to speak of the terror of fleeing fires that they could never outrun. All they could do was pray for a change in the wind.

She reminded her waiting, watching northern neighbours that catastrophe – no matter how devastating – is never just about us. No one, she testified, was reporting "the smells of burnt fur or feathers or leaves and sap or the cold hard truth of those who find the missing frozen in their last gestures of escape beneath a blanket of ashes — not even the stories reported by biologists in New Mexico who are picking up the bodies of hundreds of thousands of migrating birds in mixed flocks of warblers, flycatchers, sparrows, and finches found dead on the ground in Great White Sands with no explanation but the conjecture they died from exhaustion, forced to flee the forests before their bodies were fattened ready to make the long journeys south."

"We are saying farewell to what we love and why we stay," she testified. "The landscape of the American West is burning and we are burning too."

As she continued her testimonial, she spoke also for us, where even in September we were still under a veil of a summer of fire and thick smoke.

"We have been living a myth. We have constructed a dream. We have cajoled and seduced ourselves into believing we are the center of all things; with plants and other sentient beings from ants to lizards to coyotes and grizzly bears, remaining subservient to our whims, desires, and needs. This is a lethal lie that will be seen by future generations as, a grave moral sin committed and buried in the name of ignorance and arrogance."

She spoke for us, too, when she testified that we have mismanaged our forests by suppressing fire for decades. We, too, have ignored the wisdom of Indigenous Peoples who have understood and lived with fire in these forests for thousands of years.

"This," she testified, "is freedom unmasked. We have a right to live as we wish. Until we can't. Our reckless history of human habitation in the American West is on a collision course with the climate crisis."

Tempest Williams then went on to explain that she had been asked to write an obituary for the land – but had realized that in doing so she would be writing an obituary for all; for all the life that had been lost and can never return. But it wasn't just the other sentient beings of the land that were burned in these fires. Our innocence and denial also went up in flames.

The obituary she would write would be short. It would go something like this:

> The time came and these humans died from the old ways of being. Good riddance. It was time. Their cause of death was the terminal disease of solipsism whereby humans put themselves at the center of the universe. It was only about them. And in so doing we have been dead to the world that is alive.
>
> To the power of these burning, illuminated western lands who have shaped our character, inspired our souls, and restored our belief in what is beautiful and enduring—I will never write your obituary— because even as you burn, you are throwing down seeds that will sprout and flower, trees will grow, and forests will

rise again as living testaments to how one survives change.

It is time to grieve and mourn the dead and believe in the power of renewal. If we do not embrace our grief, our sadness will come out sideways in unexpected forms of depression and violence. We must dare to find a proper ceremony to collectively honor the dead from the coronavirus as we approach 200,000 citizens lost. We must honor the lives engulfed in these western fires and the lives we will continue to lose from the climate crisis at hand —Only then can we begin the work of restoration, respecting the generations to come as we clear a path toward cooling a warming planet.

This will be our joy.

Terry Tempest Williams went on to create that ceremony. With the ashes in hand that had fallen on the drought-cracked desert of

Utah, she raised her fist to the smoke-choked sky to honour the holy creatures, human and wild, who had lost their lives and homes to the galloping flames that burned that summer throughout the West.

Let this testament, she offered, "be a humble tribute, an exaltation, an homage, and an open-hearted eulogy to all we are losing to fire to floods to hurricanes and tornadoes and the invisible virus that has called us all home and brought us to our knees. We are not the only species that lives and loves and breathes on this miraculous planet called Earth – may we remember this – and raise a fist full of ash to all the lives lost that it holds."

Grief is love, she reminded us. To bear witness to this moment of undoing is to find the strength and spiritual will to meet the dark and smouldering landscapes where we live, and do what we can to bring back all we have taken for granted.

She then marked her heart with an "X" made of ash that said that "the power to restore life resides here. The future of our species will be decided here. Not by facts but by love and loss."

Hand on her heart, she pledged allegiance to the only home she acknowledged she will ever know.

As the fires approached that summer, that, too, was my pledge.

But though it was a year of ghostly horizons and the sun blood red in the sky, we were spared that year from the burning. To what do we owe such grace?

The fires will come again. Perhaps next year, and maybe the year after and the year after that. Is this what we want for our children? Of course not. If there was any learning in the burning, it is this: the future will come by choice or by chance. Which shall it be?

At that moment, however, we were too divided and distracted to choose or to even hear or heed the warning.

The Freedom Convoy
Wednesday, February 2, The Third COVID Year
Sunrise 8:14 AM +1 hr   Sunset 5:34 PM +1 hr
Can No One See?

This was a bad day to wake up to. The Canadian truckers' so-called "Freedom Convoy" has spread across the country with blockades not just in Ottawa but also at border crossings and now on other major roads. Police do nothing about them. Though they are in clear violation of multiple laws, there have been virtually no arrests. Here we confront a whole convoy of contradictions and enforcement inconsistencies.

As we have seen, if these were blockades organized by Indigenous Peoples to protect their land or disruptive demonstrations by activists in defence of old-growth forests, the police would have acted. They would, as we have already witnessed on television and social media, beaten the hell out of the demonstrators, then arrested them and saw that their vehicles were impounded. And laws would have been quickly passed – the very laws these truckers now violate with impunity – to prevent these kinds of disruptions from happening again.

Why is this situation so different?

We need to wake up. There is much that is very, very wrong here.

First of all, don't we see that the trucker convoy is fundamentally anti-science, anti-evidence-based decision making and, by impinging on the established rights of others, anti-democratic? Can't we see that the so-called "Freedom Convoy" is no longer about free speech; that it is full-on sedition, with the expressed aim of bringing down governments? These are not just anti-vaxxers anymore. They are anarchists. They don't even represent any-thing close to the majority of truckers. They are a splinter group that is being manipulated by the libertarian fringe represented by political parties like the People's Party of Canada and the Western separatist Maverick Party who both fuel and fund their rage.

In the places these blockades have been established, no one is amused. The mayors of Ottawa and of the border station of Coutts in Alberta claim their communities are being held hostage. In actual fact, these truckers are holding the entire country hostage.

The Canadian public is hardly innocent either. Just when we should be in a state of national outrage, Canadians for the most part just sit back and stand for this. Don't we see what we are licensing here? What example will this set for others with grievances, or sick or dangerous political agendas? When the rule of law demonstrably no longer matters, what then? Where does it stop? If motorcycle gangs decide to take over your rural town on weekends, who is going to do anything about it? If a crime ring decides to organize a campaign of regular carjackings and break-ins targeting the empty homes of weekenders, would we ignore their activities, citing that it is better to tolerate them than to risk the threat of further tensions?

Can we not see that our growing societal divisiveness and indifference are signs of a deep weakening in the moral character of our country? The American disease has fully infected us. We are losing our moral compass. Can no one see this?

Can no one see that this is the road to decline and then potentially to collapse? But this was only the beginning of the fallout nationally from the pandemic. In terms of pressures on our mountain town, the pandemic introduced new threats to our community which put into bold relief problems that were brewing long before COVID rushed onto the scene.

Fallout

Forced to Stay Home, We See Ourselves
& Our Town in Relief

There are many reasons why pandemics are becoming so much more threatening to humanity. Dramatically increasing human populations and the rapid expansion of transportation webs that interconnect within these populations offer a staggering opportunity for the epidemic spread of hitherto unimagined forms of disease.

Another reason is that we have eaten into the remote fastnesses of the natural world to such an extent that we are encountering viruses we have never met before. People are now coming into contact with ancient viral infections that have evolved over millions of years in the complex ecologies of remote rainforests. The contact would not be occurring if the deep fastness of these rainforests wasn't being disturbed.

Here's how Richard Preston put it in *The Hot Zone: The Terrifying True Story of the Origins of the Ebola Virus*, his 1994 book that focused on the outbreak of two hemorrhagic fever epidemics brought about by the Ebola and Marburg viruses in Central Africa in the late 1980s:

> Nature has interesting ways of balancing itself. The rain forest has its own defenses. The earth's immune system, so to speak, has recognized the presence of the human species and is starting to kick in.

Illness as metaphor. Though deeply entrenched in our culture, the philosophy of personal, social, ideological and environmental individuality and separateness goes counter to the interpenetrating reality of our true nature and of the nature of nature itself. While a mechanistic world view has rejected the idea that manifold realities may interpenetrate one another on frequencies and time frames hitherto imperceptible to us, more and more we are seeing that this planet is alive with non-human sentience, and an assault on one part of the Earth system can have far-reaching consequences in places far, far away from where the initial disturbance took place. COVID, as we discovered, is a classic example of the links that exist between all life. Destroy enough habitat and keep pushing long enough on the human–wildlife interface in places like China and Africa, and the next thing you know, organisms that existed 250 million years before the appearance of multi-cellular life on this planet are suddenly threatening to kill you, your family and your neighbours in Canada. And you are hardly alone in your utter vulnerability. What started out as an epidemic in China had within only weeks become a global pandemic.

It was a shock to everyone in this mountain town to wake up one March morning to find themselves in full pandemic lockdown. Many were, at first, impressed with the common goodwill and apparent adaptability of their neighbours. But then supplies began to run low and the hoarding began. Then people began resisting and then rejecting public health measures put in place to slow the pandemic until vaccines could be created to fight the virus.

People who wanted to comply with public health measures were forced to stay as much as possible in their homes and to restrict their travel. For many it was the first time they'd had to stay in town for any length of time and their first prolonged exposure to what their community was really like. Many discovered that when they had their nose rubbed in it, this wasn't the pleasant little burg it appeared to be when you could thrive on the cream you skimmed off the top between trips abroad and winters in Mexico.

Then came the disappointment and revulsion of discovering that some of those closest to you, including immediate family members, were anti-vaxxers or worse. Then the other shoe dropped. You found out that these people did not like you either, and that this was not likely to change if and when the pandemic ended. Many found they were running out of people in their town whom they wanted to be like, or even liked.

On the heels of these discoveries came the realization that not only are we unable or unwilling to effectively govern ourselves but, as the anti-vaxxers and other contrarians had shown, a sizeable number of people among whom you live were willing to go out of their way to invent their own facts and to fabricate reasons to ensure that no one will make us do so. It soon became clear that whatever public health rule was put in place would be subverted by someone. It didn't take long for this divisiveness to turn into a form of vaccination apartheid, in which opposing sides largely avoided one another so as to avoid the risk of potential disputes and possible conflict. As time wore on, it was impossible not to see that our self-entitled society was shallower and far more deeply divided than we previously imagined. The loss of civility and patience with one another in our broader society gradually became obvious. It was impossible not to see that the province in which I lived was not the open-minded place one might have superficially thought it was, but a powder keg of opposing ideology and divisiveness.

The cumulative effects of the pandemic began to mount. COVID increased the desirability of living and working at home in a quaint mountain town by orders of magnitude while at the same time demonstrating how that increased desirability would further rupture community solidarity by driving up the cost of living to an extent that even long-established residents began leaving in record numbers.

Though few saw it at the time, the lockdowns and the rising divisiveness within our own society, in combination with the acceleration of pressures on the town that existed long before the pandemic, became a form of dispossession in their own right. The legacy of COVID was not a stronger more cohesive community, it was further and deeper fallout than I could even have anticipated when I wrote *The Weekender Effect* 15 years earlier. And the fallout has not abated since.

Real Estate Values

This is the saddest, most destructive mistake
of all our sad and self-destructive mistakes, to
think that humans can degrade their habitats
and not degrade themselves.
—Kathleen Dean Moore, *Earth's Wild Music*

One afternoon, late in the second year of the pandemic, I had a conversation about localness and sense of place with one of my oldest local friends who had just returned from Prince Edward Island, where he and his wife were intending to soon move. Always thoughtful and fiercely articulate, his observations were particularly insightful that day. Reflecting on Canmore, he observed that in his view, the migration of wealth here was still less an early wave of climate change and environmental refugees seeking the last best West in which to live, and far more about pure and simple real estate speculation. In his view the sense of place established over time by long-term locals had been monetized by outside interests. The attributes of place and our local connection to them as well as our emotional relationships to where and how we lived were now, in effect, being traded on the commodities market, where the last best places are being sold at ever-rising prices to the highest bidder. Locals like himself could not afford to play in those markets that sell the only real wealth we have – the places in which we live – without our permission or even our knowledge to speculators elsewhere in the country and abroad. The only way out, it appeared to him, was to take the money the speculators offered and run. In other words, to sell out, to sever your relationship to place and re-establish it elsewhere if you could.

As my friend pointed out, it is easier for some to take the money and run than it is for others. "I grew up in Montreal," he said. "I chose this place and I can choose again. Harder for you, however, you were essentially born here and chose to stay. The diminishment and loss of place you chose to stay for and endure will be harder to deal with if only because it makes it harder for you to choose another place to go, which, of course, doesn't even figure into the extraordinary fact that we in this society are privileged enough compared to the rest of the world to take for granted that we have any choice at all."

So, I stay – I endure – and what is it that I endure? I endure the fallout from the poor choices, bad decisions and in some cases the lack of decisions of the past. And primary among the saddest and most unfortunate mistakes, as Kathleen Dean Moore has pointed out, was to think that we could continually if not relentlessly degrade where we live and not degrade ourselves. When I look back, where we started to get things wrong in this mountain town and began degrading where we live, and in so doing began to degrade ourselves, was when we no longer looked upon where we lived as a place, and began to think of it principally as a mere commodity, as real estate.

Contrary to popular local opinion, not all real estate agents are greedy monsters. If you need them to help you buy or sell a house, a good real estate agent can really help you. That said, the sector they work in could turn anyone into a monster. While some, I am sure, would try to sell you a high-end view lot on the banks of an atmospheric river, there are certainly some good ones, as we discovered, who have helped us over time. In contemplating the sequel to *The Weekender Effect*, it was invaluable to connect at least to some extent with the real estate community. Good real estate agents know stuff, and if they trust you they are happy to share it.

At the time of this writing, Canmore, where I live, was the third-fastest growing rural municipality in Canada. When I wrote this, 2019, 2020 and 2021 were record years for real estate sales in Canmore. And what was interesting was the number of properties that sold at over the asking price. In fact, demand was greatly outstripping supply. At the time of this writing there were far more real estate agents in town than there were homes for sale. The situation was such that Royal LePage, a major national real estate company with an established foothold in the Canmore market, published a circular that appeared in the mailboxes of homeowners in targeted postal codes that touted the potential advantage that sellers might have in a red-hot housing market. The flyer read like this:

LOWEST INVENTORY MARKET IN 20 YEARS

The Canmore market continues to see sale price increase into the new year. Single-family and townhomes are the most sought after and have garnered upwards of $200,000 over asking sale prices, and others with 50+ showings within days of listing.

> With mortgage interest staying at the current rate, buyers are looking to capitalize on purchasing now before the inevitable rise. If you had any thought of selling your home, now is the perfect time to list at a premium price....
>
> Please reach out to discuss how much your home could be worth, and how we can make it happen!

Leaving the issue of being in favour of or opposed to selling your home aside for the moment, one must ask, why the huge demand?

My real estate agent friends tell me that one of the reasons for such a hot market here is that Canmore is considered one of the cheaper mountain communities in Canada and North America in which to invest. Compared to similar mountain resorts elsewhere, particularly in the United States, where average property values in places like Aspen, Colorado, for example, are around US$6.5 million, places like Canmore are cheap. As one real estate agent bluntly explained, if you want to be among the global elite, Canmore offers a cheap avenue for doing so.

The problem, however, is that we don't know how to handle that here. We don't know, for example, how to deal with offshore Chinese investors who don't care about anything but capital growth. One thing that has become absolutely clear is that there is no money in building affordable housing that might have attached ownership conditions that limit the price at which they can be later bought and sold. As a result, Canmore has become little more than a trendy neighbourhood for the upwardly mobile and the retired or retiring rich. An indication that this is clearly the case is that according to my real estate friends, who know such things, there are as many as 1,000 empty weekender homes at any given moment in Canmore. And major outside development interests want to make sure there are many more.

Developers aim to make millions selling to global markets, thereby adding thousands of weekenders to the shadow population of the town. While real estate agents welcome the expanded number of properties that will be available to buy and sell in perpetuity, some are worried that a bubble is being created that won't merely burst but will be self-terminating. The moment paying millions to live in your mansion in the solitude of supposedly pristine mountain fastnesses is oversold and ruined will be the moment the bubble will burst. This without even acknowledgement of the larger elephant of climate change blundering around indiscriminately in the room in each and every real estate market.

All that said, real estate agents tell me that one should consider carefully when contemplating selling out. Many are those who sell out and regret leaving. But getting back in is not so easy. You can only take the money and run once; if you want back in, real estate prices are likely, even after only six months, to be so elevated as to make getting back in difficult if not impossible.

And, oh, another thing. Despite honourable local humanitarian intentions, bringing Syrian and more recently Ukrainian refugees to Canmore is unsustainable. They can't, any more than many locals, afford to live here, and as soon as they can acquire the means or the support they relocate to places with jobs and housing that will allow them to thrive.

Real estate agents here have explained that the popularity of second homes in this country began with the appeal of a cottage that could become a retreat from the summer heat and pollution of big eastern cities. For a long time, I didn't understand how central the idea and fact of "the cottage" were in the context of Canadian identity. As a Westerner living in the spectacular Rockies, I couldn't imagine anyone preferring a summer at a cottage on some mosquito-infested Ontario lake to a personally transformational experience in the high, clear air of some of the country's biggest rocks. As it happened, however, I was invited to speak at a water festival in Elmvale, Ontario, just minutes away from where family friends had a cottage on the sunset-facing shore of Georgian Bay. While I agreed to go when those friends offered us five days in their guest cabin, I could not imagine spending the better part of a week sitting on a beach staring at the water. But I packed up my books and off we went, and I am so very glad I did. It was one of the most inspiring and joyful experiences of my life. The place and the water spoke to me and the sunsets were stunning beyond anything I could imagine. At the end of the week, I wanted, as the owners did, to spend the rest of the summer there. We returned again for five summers. Now when someone brings up their desire go to their cottage on the lake, my immediate response is that "I get it, and I apologize, I get it," and I most enthusiastically do.

While there has always been an interest in having a summer or winter place in the mountain West, it has never had quite the cachet that cottage country gained in the East. And what is happening now bears no resemblance to the "cabin" culture that has emerged over the last century here.

The old saw that developers and real estate agents repeat again and again in mountain resort communities, where environmentalist resistance to large-scale development remains commonplace, is a tiresome one. "An environmentalist," they crow, "is someone who already has a cabin in the woods."

There are, of course, some flaws to this argument. First of all, there are no more "cabins" in the woods. They have been replaced by McMansions. Secondly, in the face of rapid development there are far fewer trees. So, absent the trees, it is difficult to have a cabin in the woods. Also, the people who now want to have property here are city people and, as Tony

Hiss famously pointed out in *The Experience of Place: A New Way of Looking at and Dealing With Our Radically Changing Cities and Countryside*, the modern city has created an entirely new kind of person. The people who now want to live here aren't interested in a "cabin in the woods." They want to remake place in the image of what they had where they came from. Instead of small houses and big yards that locals once favoured, the trend now is toward big houses that crowd right up to the neighbour's property line.

And all that goodwill and philanthropy that was supposed to attend the wealth that has been attracted here? Yes, some of the newcomers have been very generous to the local community, but there has also been a pernicious side to this generosity. When, for example, a local group wanted to raise money for an additional palliative care facility in town, they quickly discovered there was no land available for such purposes. A white knight did emerge, but their generosity had some strings attached. The landowner agreed to give the group the land they needed if the town agreed to allow five luxury homes to be built on the rest of the parcel they owned. The hitch was that the property in question was outside the urban growth boundary and within a wildlife habitat patch. This put the town in a difficult position. Was it even worth considering?

Somewhere in the middle of all this are the people who lived here before all this happened. And many of us don't like what we see, or what we see coming.

It has escaped us that everyone is paying more and more to live here. Nor is the rising cost of living here gradual and incremental. Rents, for example, can jump dramatically overnight. One bereft friend explained that the rent for the house he rented from an out-of-province owner was increased by $900 a month, or more than $10,000 a year, right in the middle of the pandemic. He was stunned. Though he was sure he could rent a place in Hawaii cheaper than he could now in Canmore, his friends were here and he was close to his son. He was desperate to stay, but he didn't know how he was going to do it.

Another well-known fellow writer noted that an empty lot on his street had just sold for $1.4 million, which would drive up the tax assessment for the house he had built for $60,000 including the price of the lot. As he told this story, he became so distraught I thought he was going to break down. It was not himself he was worried about. He already had his cabin in the woods. It was the next generation he feared for, his children and their children. "For every dollar my son saves to buy a house, prices go up three dollars. Where is the justice in that? What is happening here and so widely elsewhere," he concluded, "offends my morality, my sense of place." And there are a lot of people who feel the same way.

While many wealthy weekenders and rich retirees are oblivious to our situation, others, including federal Minister of Finance and Deputy Prime Minister Chrystia Freeland, were not afraid to tell it like it is. On April 11, 2022, Freeland called sky-high home prices "an intergenerational injustice." And that is exactly what it is. The real estate sector, however, doesn't see it that way. Soon after, the national real estate lobby mounted a campaign to oppose the imposition of new federal government regulations that would outlaw the practice of "blind bidding," in which real estate agents force buyers into a multiple-bid situation where they do not know what others are offering to pay for a property they want to buy. This practice is what is leading to homes selling for hundreds of thousands of dollars above the asking price, which, of course, is a benefit to both the seller and the real estate agent representing them. The problem, however, is that it is making home ownership out of the question for many. At the time of this writing the issue has yet to be resolved. Regardless of the outcome, though, it can hardly be disputed that it is here that sense of place slams into the dark side of real estate speculation.

Even before the 1988 Winter Olympics were held in Calgary and area, real estate agents here were buying and flipping properties. We purchased our first home from a realtor, and so did some of our friends. That appears innocent compared to what is going on today. It's time to take a peek at what hides behind the edifice of the current real estate market to see whether compromising place is in fact making the community I live in and the people I live among less than they once were. Warning: what is plaguing mountain resort communities is a symptom of a much deeper disease eating away, not just at resorts, but at the very soul of what it means to live in a democracy, increasingly infected by excessive free-market fundamentalism.

Homes No More:
What Is Behind the Wealth Storage Edifice

Matthew Soules is an iconoclast. His 2021 book *Icebergs, Zombies and the Ultra Thin: Architecture and Capitalism in the Twenty-First Century* has rocked the urban planning world. Soules is of the view that the architecture of neoliberal excess has created a stranger-than-fiction reality in which mass overbuilding is normalized; growth and decay are collapsed upon each other; owned vacancy is widespread and market volatility is destabilizing our communities. Soules likens what is happening to a collision of genres. Climate fiction meets financial fiction. Cli-fi collides with Fi-fi. How else can you explain how a collection of richly constructed but sparsely inhabited super-prime avatar destinations can come into existence in tandem with the Cli-fi that is rapidly becoming not an illusion but a terrifying reality?

Soules goes on to denounce the neoliberal policies of deregulation and privatization and the practices of financial capitalism that are now propelling the growing economic and social inequality we are seeing in our society. He then offers evidence that policies and practices allowing the purchase of properties by shell companies that conceal ownership to avoid public accountability, local specificity and taxation are harmful to the places where such investments become concentrated.

Soules takes no prisoners. He describes the thousands of vacant investment properties in the world's new super-prime luxury avatar destinations as mere "wealth storage edifices." He maintains that we have now reached the frontiers of ethical compromise that contemporary capitalism encourages. We now live in a world of avatar architecture that is owned, but empty – the owners present while at the same time absent. Soules was talking about parts of Vancouver in this context, but he might as well have been talking about the mountain town in which I live. All I have to do is look out the window to see what he is describing. If you woke up one morning to discover that some "oiligarch" had bought the house across the street that once was the home of permanent neighbours, you will know what I mean. I live here in this mountain town amidst the very avatar architecture Soules describes. I now live in a neighbourhood of owned but empty wealth storage edifices. I now live in a haunted dead space completely devoid of the dynamism of lived community vitality. How can I see these edifices popping up all around me as being anything different than what Soules has declared them to symbolize? Cli-fi and Fi-fi have had a child. That baby is named Animated Zombie Urbanism.

How extreme does the wealth gap have to become, Soules asks, before the system breaks down? He, for one, was hoping that things never return to the pre-COVID state of affairs. Sorry, Matthew, too late.

Diminishment and Loss

In no way did COVID halt the infection of Animated Zombie Urbanism that began plaguing my town long before the arrival of the pandemic. If anything, it exacerbated it. The story will undoubtedly be very familiar to those living in mountain towns like ours. The ongoing physical diminishment and loss of where we live has taken a toll on our identity as a community. It is also a huge distraction, and its legal costs alone are likely to rob Canmore of the full capacity to address the climate emergency it faces, which will slow efforts to achieve sustainability.

But despite these tensions, there are some bright spots. With respect to the capacity to understand and respond to the accelerating increase in the number, extent and duration of climate disasters, Canmore is fortunate to have one of the world's leading climate research facilities located here. When we talk about diminishment and loss, this is a capacity we don't want to lose. But here too, continually rising real estate prices pose a real threat.

Real estate practices and rising prices are not just threatening the future; they are also undoing a lot of good now. It has long been determined that once the town reached an approximation of full build-out, its economy and identity would be defined by more than building and construction. It was held that in time the town would mature into a different future. One of the most immediate ways of enhancing the character of a changing community is to elevate local knowledge and understanding of place in ways that would not only make living here richer for locals and visitors alike but would also bring benefit to all neighbouring mountain communities whose residents wanted the ongoing inspiration of ever deeper knowledge of the natural and cultural history of where they lived. The dream was to have heightened knowledge shape community identity and reputation. Establishing a university research presence in Canmore was a step toward doing just that. Building on the foundation of research that has been ongoing in the Kananaskis Valley for more than 50 years, Canmore became the centre of a high-profile joint university research laboratory with the goal of not just offering locals better understanding of the dynamics of snow, ice and climate around them but of becoming a world centre for such research, which meant bringing scientists from all over the world to live and work here.

The research goals were and continue to be lofty. What scientists have witnessed over the course of the last decade, including the growing accuracy of data, expanded understanding of Earth system function, greater knowledge and emerging common urgency are driving a revolution in the Earth sciences. Multi-spectral space-based remote sensing is making the invisible visible. Combined with careful terrestrial ground-truthing, this means what was once thought impossible may soon be possible. The Holy Grail of the hydrological sciences appears to be within our collective grasp. Because of the work of Canadian research initiatives such as the Global Water Futures Program in Canmore, integrated flood and drought prediction and forecasting and much, much more will soon be possible. As that happens, it will become possible to better predict not just potential flooding events like the one that did so much damage to Canmore in 2013, but to help others throughout the mountain West, and around the world, generate better predictive capacity in service of saving lives and reducing the damage caused by extreme weather events.

At first it worked, and Canmore was able to attract the best scientists in the world, who wanted to and could afford to live here. But that is changing. It is getting harder to attract the best researchers in the climate sciences to Canmore, because of out-of-control real estate prices. But meteorically rising house prices are only one of the unaddressed problems that came roaring back after provincial politicians officially decreed, without consulting the virus, that the public no longer needed to be concerned about COVID. Among the most pressing of these unaddressed problems is over-tourism.

Over-Tourism

I first began thinking about what an explosion in cheap travel would do to the character and nature of the mountain region in which I lived when it became clear that the perfection of the wide-bodied jet was going to change the face of tourism forever. These super-jets were time machines that could take you almost anywhere you wanted to go in the world in a day. As anticipated, the human appetite for travel was insatiable, and here foreign visitation literally skyrocketed.

As it became increasingly clear that we did not have the infrastructure to manage the annual increases in visitation, tourism became fully industrial to meet the demand. In time, traffic in and around the mountain parks became so great, and the wildlife mortality associated with it so high, that major highways had to be twinned, with fences, overpasses and underpasses constructed through the major corridors to ensure habitat connection and halt the slaughter. Few saw the irony in this. What we were in effect forced to do was to fence visitors in, and what they came to see out, in order to protect both. Machines carried the hordes to the viewpoints from which they could look out and see the iconic landscapes that tourism operators, local and regional tourism associations and provincial and federal government tourism offices proudly and relentlessly promoted abroad.

As it became clear that the tourism boom was likely to continue – albeit with an occasional bust or two along the way – I began asking travel agents and tourism promoters whether they had a moral responsibility for the impacts that over-tourism was beginning to have on the places they were relentlessly selling. The answer, of course, was *no*. If you were a travel agent, your responsibility ended when you sold a customer an airline ticket or booked a hotel for them. If you were an airline, your responsibility began and ended when a passenger got on and then got off the plane. If you were a travel promoter your job was to bring more and more people to the destinations you were selling. What these people did when they got to where they were going was not your problem. It appears now, however, that it is. As we have seen in other matters like dealing with the climate threat, if you atomize responsibility into enough fragmented transactions, you can make it disappear, and it has.

All over the world, places of great charm, cultural heritage and natural beauty are literally being overrun by uncontrolled and uncontrollable tourism. The very character of what makes them desirable places to visit is being eroded. In places like Barcelona and Venice, locals have had enough. In Barcelona, there are massive murals painted on the walls of buildings telling tourists to go home. In Venice, the city's remaining residents complain of being "suffocated" by the effects of over-tourism. Residents there are being driven out. The local population has declined by 120,000 since the 1950s. In resort communities in North Wales locals are being evicted en masse as swaths of rental properties are being converted to short-term rentals and Airbnbs. When locals in these places are not petitioning the court of public opinion to have the architects of over-tourism publicly flogged, they are demanding limits on numbers of visitors that are allowed to come; constraints on where they can go and what they can do; and greater respect for local values from travel agents, airlines and tourism promoters that send visitors their way.

Growing dissatisfaction with the fact that over-tourism was restricting the rights and freedoms of locals and undermining local landscape and cultural values was beginning to be expressed in parts of the mountain West leading up to the pandemic, but those concerns were dismissed as merely local whining and nothing was done about them, except to add more and more buses and parking to accommodate the ever-increasing hordes.

When COVID partially froze international travel, many thought the tourism sector might take advantage of the hiatus to re-evaluate the direction they were taking and consider new concepts such as regenerative tourism, which would mean bringing numbers down to Earth rather than continuing to expand capacity until its effects on local community swallowed up every reason for coming here. But that is not what happened, at least not where I live.

What happened was that visitation didn't drop; only the demographics of the visitors changed. Some international travellers simply ignored or found ways around travel restrictions and came anyway, but their numbers dropped. The hordes kept coming, but they were mostly regional visitors. Regardless of how strict the public health measures became – and in many cases in spite of them – Alberta's cities continued to empty out on weekends and the hordes poured into the mountains. Canmore, in effect, became a trendy Calgary neighbourhood, and Banff essentially became a city park. The problem then became staff. After COVID put restrictions on the ability of foreign workers to take service jobs in Canada, staffing shortages became acute. Young people, being what they irrepressibly are in nature, kept on partying together and continued to spread COVID among themselves, making it impossible for many to show up reliably for work. While one Banff operator apparently threatened to fire staff if they didn't come to work *even if they had tested positive for COVID*, staff shortages became rife. Restaurants and other businesses were forced to shorten operating hours, reduce the days they were open, or close entirely. Efforts to attract service staff from surrounding areas were confounded by the fact that the word everywhere was that Canmore was simply unaffordable as a place to live. Businesses could not find frontline staff because what they were paying was not enough to give prospective employees, even if they wanted to come, a fighting chance to be able to afford to live here. At the time of this writing that has not changed.

Meanwhile the United Conservative Party government of Alberta under the then Premier Jason Kenney announced that his government intends to double tourism to Alberta. So much for pausing and giving consideration to leading-edge ideas related to sustainable, regenerative tourism. Where, Mr. Premier, do you think these additional visitors will want to go? They sure as hell aren't going to line up to go to Raymond, Alberta. They will want to come to the mountains. We can't even handle the current fallout from over-tourism. How will we accommodate another doubling of visitation? Especially in the midst of another invasion that took us by surprise.

The Virtual Invasion

The technological solutions that became available during the pandemic have changed our lives. Communications with one another – especially in terms of business and other meetings and how and what we are able to learn – will never be the same. Until COVID, few knew of platforms like Zoom or Microsoft Teams and even fewer were using them. COVID connected us all to the virtual world, and for the existence of that world we are now mostly grateful. It allowed us to stay home and keep working, and remote work is here to stay. But there are downsides besides arriving at a situation where there seems to be one new digital device or another demanding attention until you reach the point of not knowing who serves whom. There are downsides besides finding yourself in what one of my friends called "eternal indentured zoomitude," where you spend the 35 hours you might have spent in the office in Zoom meetings and webinar updates instead. Those are challenges we can manage individually, but the other downside – the serious downside for mountain communities – relates to what happens when all those who used to work in office towers in Manhattan, New York, Toronto and other big cities around the world suddenly don't have to show up personally to work and discover they can work from anywhere and, more than that, anywhere they want.

If they're given the choice of the whole world, where will the people with the most money want to go to work? In the last best places, of course, and that is what they are doing. While they are smart, educated and often highly sophisticated people, they can pay whatever it costs to have what they want, and when they do, they will expect what they want on their terms. While they are likely to be in their new homes more often than most weekenders, they will help push prices ever higher, driving out more and more long-time locals. Fairly or unfairly, they represent the next wave of population pressure washing up the steep valley walls that surround our Western mountain towns. And it doesn't take much imagination to know where this will take us.

So, we have now reached the point in this examination of what has developed in the 15 years since I wrote *The Weekender Effect* where we can see clearly what happens when sense of place and community is reduced to place viewed solely as real estate. The results, unfortunately, begin to look like what would happen if satire and reality had a baby. All the mocking notwithstanding, the child is going to have a difficult time in the world.

We have, over time, allowed ourselves to become so habituated, if not resigned, to degradation and loss of the natural world around us that we have taken to calling what we are experiencing "the new normal." If this is the new normal, then there is nothing normal about it. There is nothing normal about one species setting into motion such a geological shift as we have done in bringing about widespread hydroclimatic change and biodiversity loss. Very simply, we should not accept this as the new normal. We must very much reject even the idea. There are other things we must reject also.

What economists can't price may cost us, in the long run, more than what they can. Foreign and outside investors have figured out that buying condos and homes in desirable mountain places is a good investment. They have also found that keeping them empty after they buy them creates local housing shortages, which pushes up prices, which benefits investors but drives out the very people whose commitment to where they live and their sense of place established the character of the communities investors are lining up to invest in. In the early 2020s, these trends have been supercharged by the COVID crisis.

Because the pandemic has shown us how many of us can work remotely, people everywhere are now looking for desirable places to relocate. We have experienced the first wave, so we know what it looks like. It is no longer a weekender effect; it is an all-out invasion. But there are other waves that are coming for which we are completely unprepared.

If COVID taught us anything it was that to be sustainable, development in the future must not only be environmentally neutral, it must also be both restorative and pre-silient. We need to be ready for anything.

Most importantly, we must be careful to avoid the fundamental error J.B. MacKinnon thinks we are making as a society: a mistake when we assume that the nature we know in our time is what it has always been, at least by any measure of time meaningful to our life-times. Each generation, MacKinnon observes, gives itself varying degrees of permission to degrade nature as they have inherited it and know it in their time and live with the consequences. Yet we are largely blind to the fact that we do this.

Denial of how much is being diminished and lost around us, MacKinnon argues, is the last line of defence against memory. It allows us to forget what we would rather not remember; then to forget that we have forgotten it; and then resist any temptation or inducement to remember. And that is why education matters so very much.

Education

At the time of this writing, the public school system in the mountain town in which I live was under siege. A local in the know explained to me that when families have children here, it is not unusual for them to stay, if they can, until their children reach the age of 5 or 6 – which is to say, school age – after which many of these families become deterred from living here by rising costs and leave. Or they wait until their kids get through high school, then they leave.

The public school system had responded to this crisis by cultivating foreign students whose families could pay a premium for a high school education abroad. At the time of this writing foreign students were still holding the public school system together. Because of COVID, however, the number of European and Latin American students was in decline. Clearly, desperate measures are necessary to keep the public system functioning, and desperate measures are what are now being taken.

The current school board has come up with a highly innovative way to create a legacy fund that will allow it to continue providing education for local students well into the future. The radical new plan involves selling some of the property the school board owns surrounding its conveniently located middle school, to be developed into housing. You guessed it: the option the school board determined would most reliably keep the public school system in Canmore solvent while ensuring that it can provide affordable accommodation for existing staff and new staff it wants to attract in the future, as well as accommodate visiting foreign students, is to sell most of the last bare land they have in their possession and keep enough to build condos that can be rented out to teaching staff so they can afford to work here. While some in the community grumble about it, the more people think about it, the more support the project appears to gain. If you can no longer afford to provide public education in the town in which you live, what do you do? Some outside-the-box thinking went into this. Too bad you have to do it, but what you do is create your own town within that town.

Leadership & Citizenship

In the midst of the pandemic, I wrote at length about the events associated with the dangerous nature of the rapidly spreading virus, but as I did, something else had started to happen that we didn't expect or anticipate. It seemed like we were using COVID as an excuse to cross a threshold that would put us on a road to giving up democracy.

Our reaction as a society to COVID, and in particular the nearly instant breakdown of solidarity with respect to common adoption of public health measures, began to tell us things about ourselves that I hoped would prove to be untrue. It soon dawned on me that there were a few things we have to fix in this society before we can effectively fix anything else. The first being the damage we have done through neglect and by way of wilful partisan intent to the fundamental institutions of citizenship and democracy.

If COVID taught us anything it was that we will not be able to address the crises of global ecological overshoot, the rapid collapse of Earthly biodiversity or the existential threat of climate disruption without first repairing and restoring our unravelling democracy.

This was hardly news among the politically informed. Dr. Thomas Axworthy was the principal secretary for Prime Minister Pierre Trudeau while he was in office between 1980 and 1984 and has been an advisor to subsequent Liberal governments in Canada ever since. In the midst of the pandemic Dr. Axworthy offered a webinar in support of Village of Love, an NGO that funded and delivered help to families caring for AIDS-orphaned children in Kenya. The title of the webinar was "Populism, Trumpism and Extreme Discord: Is Canada Immune?"

In essence, this inspired and inspiring webinar was about the politics of inclusion versus the politics of fear. Dr. Axworthy began the presentation by giving definition to populism. Populism, he offered, was a political movement that challenges the incumbent political establishment based on the claim that populists – and they alone – represent the people. As Turkey's President Recep Tayyip Erdoğan put it, "We are the people. Who are you?" Unfortunately, the brands of populism emerging today too often threaten the rule of law and the foundations of liberal democracy. Populist leaders bend the rules of democracy, and get away with it by loudly and aggressively claiming that those who oppose them don't belong.

The contemporary drivers of populism, Axworthy said, included overwhelming changes in society that lead to anxiety and fear; globalism and the decline of the middle class; the social media misinfodemic we are experiencing that has allowed populists and populism to create their own echo chambers; the capacity of social media to stoke anti-immigration sentiments and fear of others; the rise of the strongman; the purposeful cultivation of extreme political and social polarization as a response to the anxieties of the alienated; and the manipulation of that polarization as a means of further shaping that alienation.

Increasingly, opposing extremes see one another as enemies. This began with the economic collapse of 2008 but was further fuelled by second and third waves that were and continue to be a tsunami of globalization and technological change. This has led to the perception in many countries that existing governments can't deal with these anxieties, and the growing belief that their country is not going in the right direction. This, Axworthy explained, is what is inciting populism in Europe and the United States.

The degree of this dissatisfaction is dependent, of course, upon where you live. Some 58 per cent of citizens in Western countries do not think their nation is going in the right direction. Contrast that with the 94 per cent of Chinese who have watched 800 million people in their country be lifted out of poverty, and very much believe their country is going in the right direction. Elsewhere, however, young people have discovered they have to work twice as hard to have the quality of life the boomer generation before them enjoyed. And that was before COVID. Many Canadian families, Dr. Axworthy reported, are $200 a month away from financial problems. The decline of the middle class and the greater and greater concentration of wealth in the hands of fewer and fewer is in itself fuelling anger. How could it not when the top 1 per cent of the economic elite have enjoyed 27 per cent of the growth of the world's wealth?

We now find ourselves in an era where the Four Horsemen of the Apocalypse have traded their horses. Their new horses are pandemic, economic inequality, climate change and the contagious and mind-altering infodemic of social media.

Social media is now seen as a pandemic in its own right, in large measure because there are no standards of truth or objectivity in what is conveyed through social media and because for more than half of all Americans and Canadians social media is their only news source. This is why the World Health Organization recently declared that they were battling an infodemic as much as a pandemic. With good reason. It has been found that false stories and misinformation are 70 per cent more likely to be retweeted than the truth. The example that was given of this was the false story tweeted and retweeted that Pope Francis endorsed Donald Trump in the 2016 presidential election. It gets worse. Some 75 per cent of the most popular social media videos on the subject of migration are generated by anti-migration extremists.

The subject then turned to Viktor Orbán, my favourite leader of Hungary, who is proud to tell the world that he has created an "illiberal democracy," in which he now controls both the judiciary and the media. This trend is hardly new, as many historical observers have pointed out. This happened in Athens in the fifth century BC. Strongman populism is back!

Can these sensibilities infect Canada? Maybe, but we are different from the United States in fundamental ways. Canada, at the moment at least, exemplifies tolerance and the support of individual and minority rights. We actually celebrate inclusion and pluralism.

Recent polls, if you can trust them, indicate that although 24 per cent of Canadians think there are too many visible minorities, 60 per cent of Canadians don't care about ethnic makeup of immigrants. But there is a fly in the ointment. A big one. A full one-quarter of Canadians embrace populism in one form or another, which suggests it has already infected our country. The hotbeds? Certainly Alberta, where 35 per cent of the population at the time of this writing was very open to populism. This, Dr. Axworthy posited, suggests that Albertans were, when I wrote this, the least happy Canadians. But it isn't just Alberta that is unhappy. There are 6,600 online channels, pages, groups and accounts across several social media platforms where Canadians and who knows who else spread extremist views to 11 million other Canadians.

That said, the number one driver of populism in Europe and the United States is immigration, which is not the issue in Canada that it is in Europe or the United States. One reason for this is that in our electoral system it is very difficult to win on an anti-immigrant platform in the heavily populated suburbs of Montreal or Toronto, which are largely comprised of immigrants.

There is another factor that separates Canada from, for example, the United States. Voters in Canada are a lot more fluid in changing their party allegiance than in the United States. Only 26 per cent of the voting public in Canada are as polarized and committed to their party's platforms and ideology regardless of circumstances as in the United States. But again, this is important to watch. While there may be less left–right polarization in Canada than in the United States, we need to remind ourselves that one-quarter of the population of Canada is prepared to forget or forsake democratic norms in favour of a high degree of populist leadership. This is particularly the case in Alberta and Saskatchewan, where populist leaders are stoking fear and fuelling rage about their circumstances within cooperative federalism by constantly pointing out to their constituency how the rest of the country – and in particular Ottawa – isn't paying attention to their economic and other woes and doesn't care about them.

We can't ignore that the alt-right has a nucleus in the United States. Here in Canada, however, the Charter of Rights and Freedoms still prevails. Yes, we have pockets and ripples of populism in Canada to which we must pay close attention. Axworthy concluded with recommendations for how Canada should respond to the threat of the populist infection spreading north.

First, we should not be complacent. Extreme right groups must be closely monitored. They must be seen to be as great a threat to national security and stability as ISIS or Al-Qaeda.

Secondly, the torrent of disinformation on social media must be recognized as a national and international security threat.

We need a Royal Commission on National Security to recommend manufacturing capacity be maintained to ensure local supply on critical materials and supplies we need in the face of a global public health catastrophe like a pandemic or similar emergency.

We cannot just focus on big cities in our response to the challenges we will face in the post-COVID world. We also need to distribute support evenly to smaller centres and rural areas.

In the dialogue that followed with participants, Dr. Axworthy also offered that the power of the prime minister has gone too far. Committees examining national issues should have the power to elect their own chairs, and all who are elected should strive to make addressing the nation's challenges as non-partisan in discourse as possible.

In the broader discussion with participants in the webinar, the same question kept emerging. How do we prevent the growing threat of populism from undermining democracy in Canada? Tom Axworthy's response: we must start with a mindset that refuses to demonize the other. All opinions must be respected. We have to be tough on preventing ourselves from moving into and accepting extremism. We must recognize that freedom of expression is critical. We must push back as quickly as possible on assaults on that freedom so that we don't fuel further divisiveness. That means we must come down hard on the elected representatives at all levels who can't be civil and cannot be tolerant. Domestic terrorism should be as great a concern as international terrorism. We must recognize that left-wing and right-wing populism are equally dangerous to our democracy, but for different reasons.

Evangelical Christians are the mainstay of the Republican party extremism in the United

States. We must pay attention to this trend here in Canada.

We also need to work out how we can maintain the critical role of journalism and local opinion in the age of the internet. We need to find a vaccine for the misinfodemic that has insinuated itself into the stable of horses that the Four Horsemen of the Apocalypse have ridden behind us into the Anthropocene.

In the meantime, populism is an ill we must be fully on guard against in Canada. It would be helpful in this to be reminded of the words of our national anthem. There are and will always be things we must stand diligently and urgently on guard against that threaten the heart of our hard-won freedoms and national identity. This time it is not an external threat – or at least not primarily. It is an internal threat. The threat is the one posed by the very technology that was billed as possessing the greatest potential in all of human history to create the kind of global discourse that would bring about lasting social justice and equality. That technology has failed us. Social media has now gone rogue. It has been appropriated by populist, libertarian and foreign nationalist interests that now dangerously threaten the very foundations of liberal democracy, not just in Canada but around the world. It is an epidemic in its own right – one more threat against which we need to vaccinate ourselves.

There are ripples of populism in Canada but, as yet, no wave. We need to keep it that way. O Canada, we stand on guard for thee.

We need to be looking deeply into the foundations of our democracy to find where the cracks are; and when we do we find that atomized jurisdiction has grown to be a serious threat to our ability to fix any of the common problems we face, whether at the municipal, regional, provincial or national level. A good example of this is how fractured jurisdiction is making it impossible to effectively address the accelerating threat of climate disruption.

In 2021, I was honoured to be able to sit in on a Federation of Canadian Municipalities (FCM) webinar on meeting national goals for carbon dioxide emissions reductions as prescribed by the Paris Climate Accords. What the webinar demonstrated was a great deal of goodwill but limited capacity to achieve emissions reductions targets at the municipal level because of structural obstacles to meaningful action.

The webinar was organized by ICLEI, the International Council for Local Environmental Initiatives, of which FCM is a member. The goal, the moderator pointed out in the introduction, was to aim at two levels of emissions reduction targets: at the level of municipal operations and then at the level of broader community emissions reductions.

The FCM plan calls for net zero emissions by 2050, with 90 per cent of the target reached through direct emissions reductions and 10 per cent through offsets using 2005 as the baseline.

From the webinar it appeared that most larger municipalities employ their own token sustainability or climate resilience officers. I say token because, as the webinar unfolded, the extent to which their hands were tied in pursuit of their nearly impossible task was slowly revealed.

To their great credit, however, the sustainability officers on the panel clearly recognized the cognitive dissonance between the goals and what municipalities can realistically achieve. Net zero by 2050, they argued, is simply not achievable under ossified municipal and provincial governance structures. Climate emergency declarations up the ambition but don't make the targets any easier to achieve. The easiest targets to achieve are those linked to municipal operations that are under the control of town councils and administrations. Beyond that, broader targets, that require support from local citizens and provincial and federal governments, appear almost impossible to achieve in the necessary time frame.

Why? While the federal government may have aspirations on the world stage to promise deep emissions cuts by 2030 and more by 2050, many provincial governments are not on board with federal ambitions. Some provinces, like Alberta, are actively hostile to the very idea of climate change and have vowed to stand in the way of any federal climate action plan. Many municipalities find themselves in the middle of this tension and their climate action ambitions hampered by jurisdictional discontinuities.

Achieving these targets also assumes a stable society and a common commitment among the majority of citizens to acting on the climate threat. That common commitment doesn't exist in many parts of this increasingly internally divided country.

Achieving emissions reduction targets also assumes at least some control over growth.

The growth imperative, however, remains deeply embedded in our national psyche. Unfortunately, support for endless growth and effective climate action have difficulty being in the same room at the same time. The tension between the two is glaringly obvious. How does a town like Okotoks, Alberta, for example, consider emissions reduction targets anything but aspirational when the town's plan is to more than triple its population to 60,000 in the coming decades? Canmore could eventually double its population, creating problems that not only make it difficult to meet emissions reduction targets but will change the entire physical and social character of the town. These examples seem like nothing in comparison to the challenges other municipalities face. The population of Toronto, for example, is projected to double by 2041. Fighting development is difficult.

There is also the problem of local jurisdiction. Canmore, for example, has set an emissions reduction target of 30 per cent below a 2015 baseline by 2030. It doesn't look anything like an ambitious target until one realizes the challenges in achieving even this modest goal. One problem is that, while the town may be able to reduce its own operational emissions, literally hundreds of thousands of outsiders bring their carbon dioxide emissions from wherever they live and emit them here. Then there is the nearby Lafarge cement plant in Exshaw. Canmore's annual emissions are around 250,000 tonnes a year. The cement plant emits 1,250,000 tonnes a year, and Canmore, because it has no jurisdiction there, and because the cement-making process involves cooking the carbon dioxide out of limestone, can't do anything about it.

The FCM's challenge to municipalities to compete with one another in "a race to zero" is good in theory, but the idea needs to be refined. There is a lack of consistency. The baselines for establishing municipal targets, for example, are all over the map. In one municipality it is 2005, in another 2007 and in another 2013.

Clearly, the Federation of Canadian Municipalities needs to work on changing federal and provincial legislation that stands in the way of effective climate action at the municipal level.

So where do we go from here?

Councils pass resolutions that their municipality will reduce emissions by up to 50 per cent by 2030 and achieve net zero by 2050. Easy commitments to make. But without meaningful action the declaration of a climate emergency is not only just "happy talk," it is just kicking the climate can down the road. Unless backed by effective, immediate action, declaring a climate emergency is dangerous because it gives the impression of dealing with the problem when you are not.

Many who pass such motions know they won't be on council that far into the future and therefore won't be blamed if those targets are not achieved.

And here we arrive at the most important message that emerged from this webinar. Without near-term targets, elected officials cannot be held accountable for the failure to meet the longer-term goals. It is easy for political leaders to promise that we will somehow achieve these targets by 2050, but what are they doing NOW to get there? This puts into relief the larger challenges of municipal governance. Creating targets is just show unless support can be generated in the community to measurably achieve them.

How do you get social buy-in in the midst of all the other complaints and issues citizens continually make and raise? How do you get business support to push and meet the targets? Targets also have to be informed by the realization that the climate threat is not static. We are facing rapidly changing and accelerating climate circumstances. What we thought were planetary carbon sinks are now turning because of warming into carbon sources.

The conclusion at which I once again arrived as the webinar came to a close was that the biggest problems we face as a society are twofold. While many of the problems in communities like mine are, at least in part, of their own making, the solutions are often outside their jurisdiction to address. The laws of the land do not favour locally established limits to development or environmental restraint. They exist to serve market and economic forces. The second problem is a lack of urgency in addressing potentially existential threats. Where is the urgency? There is a widespread sense that once the targets are set that they are somehow going to miraculously achieve themselves. And wishful thinking has it also that they will do so without any fuss or disruption of the status quo. Good luck on that one.

Not enough is happening in terms of climate action at the municipal level, and what is happening is not happening fast enough. And it can't happen without massive societal change. For all our good intentions, it appears at the moment that we are not smart enough, or organized enough, to address the climate threat. It is not that these targets and the current plans to achieve them are not enough. Worse than that, they are presently so weak, and the capacity to achieve them so hamstrung, that we might as well do nothing.

The climate is coming at us fast and municipalities are already getting hammered, with worse to come with each passing season. It is only a matter of time before municipalities will no longer be able to bear the cost of extreme weather events, and it will, at that point, be too late to aim for targets that are increasingly beyond their grasp and capacity.

To avoid disastrous consequences, immediate year-by-year targets are absolutely essential. To achieve those targets, municipalities need all the citizen support they can possibly get to set and meet those targets. If there ever was a time for fierce, relentless, informed citizenship and visionary leadership, it is now. How can we elicit that kind of citizenship? Given the current state of informed citizenship in Canada, it won't be easy.

The mountain town in which I live is like Italo Calvino's *Invisible Cities*. It is not one coherent place but many different and often competing places existing simultaneously. Because it is now many places all at once, there is nothing logical about governing it. In such circumstances political and administrative leadership becomes a huge concern. The old political formulae won't work in a world of divided constituents and jurisdictional fragmentation and growing political territoriality. Electing a mayor who promises everyone everything will inevitably lead not to improved governance but to more divisiveness and citizen alienation. Electing one-issue candidates and slates will ultimately yield the same disappointing results.

Nor will creating a phantom shadow civic government, as this community has attempted to do, bring any better results. You are just replacing one form of failed governance with another. It is exactly through such measures that governance in communities collapses and you arrive at little or no capacity to deal effectively with surprise public health threats like COVID, or threats imposed from without like Earth system overshoot and climate disruption. The risk in being unable to manage such threats is not that the community in which you live will explode; the danger is that it will implode.

To get back on track we have to neutralize the divisiveness and clear the waters of democracy, especially at the community level. That can't be done without energized citizen commitment and stronger political leadership.

We have examples in this country of how that can be done. In the first decades of this young century, the Northwest Territories realized that the top-down way of governing wasn't working. If it was to address the challenges of a rapidly changing climate and fit somehow into a world in which established norms were unravelling, it had to find ways to co-create anew the very structures of political discourse and decision making. A new generation of highly committed leaders looked for cracks in the foundations of their democracy and found many. Instead of encouraging and trusting locally generated solutions to community problems, the government instead hired consultants at four or five times the cost to arrive at exactly the same solutions locals long before had identified. They fixed this crack by co-creating the objectives of consultants, if it was agreed that they were needed.

The goal soon became to make communities the architects of change, not victims of change. They quickly found unity in community, and when the federal government was ready to devolve many of what previously were federal powers over the territories, the territorial government was ready. Through careful negotiation of the terms and conditions of devolution, the people of the Northwest Territories were able to crack the ceiling of jurisdiction and regain control of where they live.

The unexpected lesson we learn from the Northwest Territories example is that full governance reform is not out of the question. A population of citizens similar to that of the mountain valley in which I live demonstrated that there's nothing in the Canadian federalist political structure that makes the kinds of reform necessary to adapt successfully to climate change or any other threat impossible. It is no longer possible to say that such levels of reform are out of the question because of legislative, legal, policy or political obstacles.

This should be viewed as good news. Governments don't have to be limited to playing around the edges of reform; they can make real change happen. Sustainability is not an impossible goal. The legal powers are in appropriate hands, and necessary policy avenues do exist to make such changes in governments possible. What is needed is leadership.

Time is something we never get back. But if we have learned anything from COVID and its attendant events, it is that we have to concentrate now on what holds us together; otherwise, we are lost.

Traffic

Perhaps the most irritating but also the most symbolic fallout from the threats to place and sense of place that I identified in *The Weekender Effect* are the impacts associated with an explosion in traffic, not just in vehicular traffic, though those have been overwhelming, but also in wilful adversarialism, misinformation, disinformation and orchestrated political divisiveness. The full measure of these impacts is the increase in total noise generated by buses, cars, motorcycles, trucks, trains, planes and helicopters and the noise generated by television, radio and social media. And what a cacophony it has become.

The biggest problem is congestion. There simply isn't enough room on the roads or in our minds for all this traffic. There are more and more days and times, especially but no longer limited to weekends, when there is no point trying to get downtown. And forget going anywhere on the last day of a long weekend. It simply takes too long and is too frustrating to attempt. Better to pick off-peak times and days to shop for groceries and supplies. This is new, but one adjusts.

Logically, the Town's response is to do everything to make our community car-free, but not everyone can ride bicycles, and although it has yet to occur to Town planners, Canmore in Alberta is not Victoria in British Columbia. Hello! Have you noticed that the Northern Hemisphere still retreats from the sun for half the year, and that, though milder than in the past, there remains this small matter of winter? Winter here can be six to seven months long. And despite global warming, it still has a bite.

To the Town's credit, however, it has introduced an ever more efficient public transit option. And they have added charm to it. While the neighbourhoods through which these buses wend, collecting passengers along the way, are often named after the animals and landforms they replaced, these vehicles are wrapped with images of the wildlife species we don't want to displace, such as deer, wolves, bears, bighorn sheep and even lynxes. Absent in the fleet, however, is a bus bearing an image of a mountain caribou. They are extirpated, gone. That fact, however, makes the move to efficient public transit even more important.

While the move to a bicycle culture will undoubtedly reduce vehicular traffic to some extent, bicycles themselves are also a form of traffic. Since bylaws no longer require cyclists to dismount at pedestrian crosswalks, the growing number of cyclists in the town has been accompanied by a growing sense that the rules of the road no longer apply to them. Cyclists routinely swerve in and out of traffic at speed and run red lights with apparent impunity. While responsibly sharing the road with cyclists has always been a given in this community, this long-standing obligation has been turned on its head. Motorists hope and pray that cyclists will share the road with them. It is in their interest to do so. As one redneck wit put it, "They do so howl when they get stuck in the wheel well of my Dodge Ram."

While it may have had a somewhat ameliorating effect in town, the rise of the bicycle culture has not reduced traffic on backcountry trails. At the time of this writing, E-bikes were expected to permitted to go on backcountry mountain bike trails in the coming spring. No one appears to have figured out yet that electric motors are still motors. What we are permitting is motorized vehicles on our mountain trails. Also being piloted are commercial E-bike tours on the same mountain trails. There appears to be confusion over what is "good" motorized and what is "bad." What will be permitted next? Motorcycles and quads? Having already turned our precious mountain landscapes into gymnasiums, we are now mechanizing and monetizing place. Once again, we are selling ourselves out.

The true extent of our traffic problems became clearly apparent on Friday, August 13, during the second year of the pandemic. In the late afternoon of that day, a grass fire near the highway at Dead Man's Flats decided it wasn't happy just being a grass fire and leapt into the adjacent forest. It was deemed necessary to close both of the eastbound lanes of the Trans-Canada Highway to give firefighters room to fight the blaze. Despite the fact that fire smoke had filled local skies all summer, a lack of emergency preparedness quickly became obvious. The highway quickly became a 50-kilometre-long parking lot that extended from Dead Man's Flats, west to Canmore, all the way to Banff.

Soon every avenue of ingress or egress from town was bumper to bumper with people trying any way they could to get around the blockage. Traffic in town, wherever you turned, soon became completely gridlocked. Vehicle movement in the entire valley was paralyzed and literally came to a standstill. Though I have seen and unwittingly been trapped in some big traffic snarls, especially in cases of accidents in the eastbound lanes on the final day of a long weekend when it seems that half the population of Calgary is on their impatient way home after a few days in the mountains, I had never seen anything like this.

What transpired that day must be seen as a turning point. It should have been obvious that those were the exact conditions that in extreme fire hazard could lead to disaster. Had the fire got out of control, hundreds of people could have died in their cars. And yet there was no notification on the Town of Canmore's emergency warning system telling people what was happening and what to do and directing people who weren't already trapped in the traffic to stay home. There wasn't even a police presence.

It took nearly two hours to travel the few blocks from the edge of the congestion to where I can turn at last onto the quiet street where I live, and hours for the jam to unravel. From the deck of my house at midnight, I could see the red of flames reflected in the clouds of smoke still rising from the wildfire. Our house had been spared this time. But only this time. Welcome to the future.

Our local traffic woes have not been helped by the fact that, even with a staggering budget, the traffic engineering department of the Town appears incapable of designing and constructing a functional major intersection.

It is hard to change direction in heavy vehicular, political and existential traffic. We are hardly alone in facing such challenges. We are, in fact, in some prestigious company.

Fallout Elsewhere

We are by no means the first or only mountain community to have these troubles. Canmore is downwind and downstream from Canada's premier mountain town – a town known around the world for its natural beauty and attractions.

Just before the pandemic began, an exhibition was mounted, or I should say remounted, at Banff's famous Whyte Museum of the Canadian Rockies celebrating the 25th anniversary of a photographic exhibition of mine called *This Business of Banff* that explored local visions, at the time, of what Banff's future might or should be. The idea behind remounting the exhibition was that it would provide an opportunity to see how closely those visions approximated what had happened in reality over the following quarter-century.

The exhibition put contentious local issues into ongoing historical relief, not just related to Banff or neighbouring Canmore but also to resort communities throughout the mountain West, and beyond.

For me Banff had become a poster child for the collateral damage that can happen to well-meaning people who care about place but accidentally find themselves in a head-on collision between idealism and money. Twenty-five years after the initial conversation, the people of Banff still seemed unable to agree on what to do with all they had.

I had left the final word in the exhibition to a local named Mike McIvor, who remembered a time when the town of Banff existed for the park, not the other way around. The town then was expected to meet the basic needs of locals and visitors without creating a demand for the unnecessary, the frivolous or the trivial. The principal measure of progress with respect to Banff, in Mike's estimation, was the degree to which visitors could come to understand that the town should not be viewed as the end of a journey, but the beginning.

That leads us to perhaps the most telling lesson we can learn from this 25-year-old exhibition, and here it is: 25 years later there is no shared definition of what progress means, and an almost complete absence of a commonly held vision of what Banff might be at its future and ultimate best.

Alternatively, it could be that what exists now may be what Banff actually and actively wanted to become over time. I know too many good people there, however, who work for the Town or Parks Canada, to believe that for a moment. Contrary intentions notwithstanding, it appears Banff remains ill with a debilitating local infection that affects communities that permit inside and outside economic interests to sell the unique nature and character of where and how you live to ever-increasing numbers of outsiders without adequate regard for social consequences or environmental limits.

It appears that many other mountain towns are at risk of picking up this infection. A full cure is not possible in the short term. At the moment, Banff has to live with this condition. If it, and we, want this condition to remain tolerable over time we may have to swallow a bitter pill. We may have to somehow limit growth and access, at least until we can figure out what we want to become at our future and ultimate best.

Though many would like to think otherwise, the frontier era in the West is over. Our mountain towns in Canada are trapped in an exhausted past. We are at risk now of falling victim to our own pathological greed and morbid individualism. Some communities, however, are waking up to the fact that they are heading down the wrong path to a future they neither planned nor welcome. Some, like Canmore, don't know how to turn back. Others see where places like Canmore are headed and are trying to put on the brakes. They see that if they don't put on the brakes current and future pandemics and climate change will do it for them. It is not too late for places like Kimberley, Fernie, Rossland, Nelson, Kaslo, Revelstoke, Golden in the interior, or for coastal communities like Tofino and even Whistler. My warning to these wonderful places is, don't let what happened to us happen to you. If you are on that path, TURN BACK, IT'S A TRAP! One might argue that this warning is somewhat disingenuous in that it is offered by someone who already has a cabin in the woods in a mountain town that has everything everyone wants. But if you take a wrong path and arrive at the wrong place, isn't it your duty to warn others not to take that path?

But why limit the warning to the West? Until they wake up to the economic and physical limits of endless growth, aren't other places equally vulnerable to a widening gap in equality, greater divisiveness and the alarming acceleration of Earth system deterioration and climate change? Other last best places to live have already figured this out. The citizens of Orillia, Ontario, have rejected a growth plan created and supported by elected officials because they did not believe the process through which the plan was developed was democratic at the local level.

Many communities are approaching the periphery of their municipal boundaries. Cities like Hamilton, Ontario, whose citizens like where they live, have identified sprawl as the enemy and decided to draw the line on growth. Citizens there know that under the provincial Municipal Act, which favours development and developers, drawing that line will be tedious, expensive and time consuming – but, in their minds, enough is enough.

These are Canadian examples. If you really want to see how far the boundaries of the debate over the future of the last best places can be stretched, one must turn to what is happening in the American West.

Whitefish is considered to be one of the last best places in Montana. There, according to local newspapers, a billionaire family, ironically from Canada, made their presence known locally by buying a 260-acre property adjacent to the Whitefish Mountain Resort on Big Mountain. They then bought nearly 126,000 acres of forested timberland west of Kalispell, land that, though previously privately owned, was where generations of Montana families had been allowed to hunt and fish under a succession of corporate owners that maintained an open-gate policy. At the time of this writing, the family owned 18 per cent of all the private land in Flathead County and intended to own much more in the future. Though the family claims that the objective of their ownership is conservation and that residential development is not the goal, many local Montanans are nervous.

Meanwhile, the Whitefish city council was in a fierce debate regarding a gateway development at the base of Big Mountain Road that included a proposal to build 380 units of new housing. Sensitive to growth pressures and the disposition of a vocal public who made the case that "the kinds of people who live here aren't the kind that can hire lawyers to come and speak," as one citizen put it, five of the six councillors turned down the application.

The Americans could have taught us much if we had listened. Influential people who have visited from Telluride in Colorado to attend the Banff Mountain Film Festival have been warning Canadians for 20 years of what was coming our way. At the time those warnings were beginning to be sounded, Banff also had the opportunity to seriously pursue a heritage tourism strategy – a strategy for the evolution of what decades later would be called restorative tourism. It rejected that strategy as the foundation of its future. Instead, it chose hardball tourism sector lobbying and self-terminating industrial tourism as its model.

The US continues to offer us lessons. At the time of this writing, Vail, Colorado, where the average house price is reported to be US$6.5 million, appeared to have become a victim of its own success. The famous resort was embroiled in a big controversy over the price of ski passes relative to the quality of service. After record sales of reduced-priced ski passes, Vail was mired in what *Outside Online* reported as an "endless barrage of complaints, social media vitriol and negative news stories." Complaints centred around congestion, long chairlift lines and reduced operations. Local newspapers were hammering Vail for its huge crowds and the decline in customer service. Customers in droves are petitioning for refunds. One of the criticisms heard most often was that Vail's management was ignoring feedback from its boots-on-the-ground employees, who were on the frontline of the problems. Meanwhile, in the valley floor, a huge debate was underway about ways in which an explosion in the number of people living in their vans might be managed. Many of those living in their recreational vehicles said they did so because they could never be able to buy a house or even afford to pay ever-higher rents without taking on two or more of the jobs available to them in the service sector. This issue was only one of many linked to the growing economic and social equality crisis that has begun to tear America apart.

The extent of the inequality that exists in the United States was put into clear relief by a recent analysis of Internal Revenue data as it pertains to Jackson Hole, Wyoming. The analysis found that when it came to the wealthiest Wyoming locales, it was no exaggeration that Teton County was in a class of its own. The average household income in Jackson

Hole, at $312,442, stood all alone in the top tier. The next 62 highest-income counties in the United States together comprised the next tier, followed by the remaining 3,000 or so other counties, boroughs and parishes.

The analysis of the IRS data also showed there were some troubling trends afoot in Teton County. Some 95 per cent of businesses reported that the community's workforce housing crisis had made it difficult to find and keep staff.

The same trends are emerging in high-end resort destinations in the United Kingdom, ski resorts in Europe and the last best places in Australia. In Wales, locals complain that the British visitation and presence has become so overwhelming that it is robbing them not just of place, but of language and culture. Wales has introduced a second-home tax to turn the heat down.

Examples exist widely indicating that highly attractive places to live and visit need to prepare to protect themselves from the threat of economic, cultural and environmental dispossession.

If what is happening elsewhere proves anything it is that we cannot give up on creating the West we want. We should never lose sight of the fact that the potential always exists to create a better world out of the one we have.

What we are engaged in – and have been engaged in for the last 25 years – is nothing less than a struggle to redefine our dominant mythology. And I know that there are still people here who want to create that mythology.

What we need most urgently is a fresh dream of who we are – one that tells us how to act; new stories about taking care of what we have that drive us to take appropriate action. As part of this new narrative, we also need to create a new sense of time that extends forward to include future generations. Right now, finding that story may be our most urgent need for collective action.

So where in this can we look for hope? As it happens, it is all around us.

Hope

Bridging the Generational Divide

So where is the hope in all this? Well, actually there is a lot more hope than might immediately be obvious. But before we talk about where hope resides, let's talk about what hope is and what it means.

One of my colleagues, Pedro Peres-Neto, is of the view that hope is an individual path that takes place in a hall of mirrors in which we see reflected the hopes of others. In this way hope can become a communal path to understanding the hopes of others. This matters, because generating public hope demands that our hope mirror the hope of the multitude of others with whom we share this life. We both agree, however, that hope is merely wishful thinking unless it is accompanied by clear intention and supported by action. So, if we are looking for hope, let's start by looking in the mirror.

What do you do when you wake up in the morning and discover that you are a functional part of the most dangerous culture on Earth, one that has contributed more than almost anything else to a planetary crisis of such dimensions that it threatens to bring down not just itself but a large and vital part of the system that makes life possible on the only home we have? What do you do when you discover that it is not just your generation that is stupefied by that realization but the one that will follow yours? The first thing you do is listen to that generation. And together you look for the truth.

So, if truth is to ultimately matter, what do I hold to be true? I believe what young people are telling us. National Public Radio in the United States recently reported the results of a survey of 10,000 young people in ten countries. Eight of every ten surveyed told researchers that people have failed to take care of the planet. Eight of ten also stated that, for them, the future is frightening. *Half thought humanity was doomed*; and four out of ten claimed to be reluctant to have children because of their fear of climate change. Keeping these emotions down, it was noted, would be like trying to push an inflated ball under water.

Young people are right to be frightened. If we do not do the right thing – right now – in terms of anticipating climate change impacts on future water security we could soon live in a world so changed that much of the history, literature and culture that has enriched our lives may no longer be relevant, because the very landscapes upon which our heritage was established will have changed. The places that we so love, the places in which we have established our identity and sense of place, may no longer be as we knew them. And we as people will not be the same.

Indigenous Peoples know that addressing these matters is a matter of cultural survival. If there is no future for Indigenous Peoples and values, there is no future for anyone. While the next generation may see that, many of the rest of us don't see it yet. The fact is that addressing these threats is a matter of cultural survival for all. That said, I firmly believe that we can understand the global problem we face and act in ways that will benefit the lives of all. And so, as it happens, do a lot of younger people.

There is a general sense in some circles that the current boomer generation has had a falling out with the generations that will succeed them. While there are certainly issues with respect to intergenerational equity on many levels, I don't believe the gap is as big as some maintain it to be. As a measure of that belief, I would like to share answers to fundamental questions posed to nine participants on an amazing webinar celebrating Earth Day organized by Creatively United and the Gail O'Riordan Climate and the Arts Legacy Fund in Victoria on youth perspectives on climate change, the pandemic and the future. It is important to note that these participants ranged in age from 12 to 19. The participants included Katia Bannister, Emma-Jane Burien, Kylan Glass, Jamie Hunter, Ella Kruus, Samantha Lin, Grace Sinats, Julia Zirnhelt and Rebecca Hamilton.

What do you suggest we should be doing in support of creating caring communities?

We were planning at this point to be working on a green new deal municipalities campaign – trying to get municipalities to implement a green new deal. But everything has changed of course.... [This is] the biggest moment of change since World War II. We recognize that this needs to be a moment where we shape the change that's going to come out of this and define what our world is going to look like after COVID-19. The world we want is one that prioritizes justice for all people and recognizes the need for a bold climate action, because if we don't push that change and if we don't create that vision then other people with values significantly different from ours will. We're trying to explore how to do that through getting involved in various pushes. We see a key goal of ours as giving agency to youth and getting youth involved. So, a big part of what we do is bringing youth into the movement and giving them the skills to organize. We're all learning together because they don't teach you this stuff in high school. And so we're also spending this time trying to restructure and figure out how we can bring a lot more people in.

What do you think is the most important thing that people should know about COVID-19 in relation to the climate crisis and the Green New Deal?
The most important thing for us to know about the COVID-19 pandemic is that it is

more related to climate change and globalization than most people actually think. Due to globalized deforestation, significant amounts of carbon are being released into the atmosphere, furthering the greenhouse effect that is causing a global rise in temperature. Organic plant matter sequesters anthropogenic carbon emissions such as those due to logging, development and urbanization, which is critical in mitigating the effects of climate change in order to achieve carbon neutrality. Carbon is being released into our atmosphere at an accelerating rate. Humidification is the plant process that stores carbon and it depends on actively growing plants. When plant matter is destroyed, for example when a tree is cut down, the carbon sequestered by that plant is released into the atmosphere. The main cause of deforestation is the conversion of forests into agricultural land. The destruction of landscapes and ecosystems, together with urbanization and the acceleration of the alteration of natural landscapes, has been linked to the emergence of infectious diseases as they spill over from other organisms and are transmitted to humans. Some 60 per cent of emerging infectious diseases that affect humans are zoonotic and more than two-thirds of those originate in wildlife. It is the alteration of natural landscapes and ecological degradation that has led to humans eating down the food chain, resulting in the emergence of viruses like COVID-19. Our species has created the circumstances that have allowed for the globalized emergence of COVID-19. I think it is time for us to finally re-evaluate our urbanization and development practices and make serious changes. Covid-19 is not a coincidence. It is a direct by-product of our unsustainable actions.

What inspires you to do the work you do?
Anything you look at in the world – any part of society – is threatened by the climate crisis.

If we don't do anything about it almost everything that we love is at risk, so when you look at all that, how can we not do anything about it? We keep saying let's go back to normal as if that's something that we want to have. We don't want to go back to normal, because normal was the world that was sleepwalking toward the edge of a cliff. I think we should do everything we can to avoid going back to normal. Obviously, there are things that we're going to want to go back to. We are going to want to go back to seeing people and being around people, to building that physical community up around us again. But there are other things that we definitely do not want to go back to, so I think it's really important that everyone thinks about the world that they want to create in the future after this pandemic. Think about what elements of normality we want to carry through and what elements we want to adapt and change into the future.

What do you think about lowering the voting age to 16?

I'm actually a campaigner for the Vote 16 BC campaign and I am thus really interested in lowering the voting age to 16. We think it gives youth a voice in politics to start seeing some of these government changes that we want to see happen. We think there will be a massive increase in voter turnout when you start engaging with youth. Other places have lowered the voting age provided voter education is offered in school. They have seen a massive increase in the people who come out when they're younger and then stay voters for the rest of their lives. So, it's a more accurate representation of our voting body.

Do you think corporations should be liable if they are involved in decisions that threaten your future?

I absolutely think that corporations should be held to account for the decisions that they are making that are literally taking people's lives all across the planet. I think that our shared story as a society and our cultural values need to shift. It's morally reprehensible to be a person or a part of a body whose entire business model is polluting the world. We need shared values that we all hold that are part of our legal system.

What advice would you give to someone who wanted to become involved in the matters we have been discussing?

Two of the biggest things I've learned about how change gets created in the world is that first of all everything happens in community; and that we only have power together and that change happens when people come together and share their talents and their ideas and create something bigger than themselves. No one individual is going to be able to change everything. There's so much that needs to be changed that we need everybody, and everybody has a role. Because there's so much that needs to change the most effective thing any person can do is whatever is most joyful to them, because what is joyful is sustainable.

What can adults, other organizations and elected officials do to support you?

In terms of the monetary situation: to say it bluntly, events cost a lot of money and we don't have many other means other than out of our own pockets to get that money. A lot of our expenses were just coming from our pockets. Money is always a support for us because then we can choose what we need it for. On our website we are planning to have a really comprehensive breakdown of what exactly we're spending your money on, just so it's very trustworthy and very transparent.

◆◆◆

The other thing I'd like to bring up is the importance of older people standing up for younger people in their circles. There are so many derogatory comments that are made about youth and assumptions about young people that are really not true like not being educated, not being motivated, just skipping school. These things are not true. So being an older person it's really important to younger people if you can say that's not true and direct people who say things like that to young people. We want to talk to those people and say "hey, have a conversation with me, see what I'm really like before you make those assumptions."

How do we prevent sliding back into the old normal once the pandemic has been managed?

We can prevent sliding back into the status quo by thinking about ways that we can bridge the gap between acknowledging what we know is wrong and then creating systems that will bring people together and uplift voices that are not typically heard and make our political and our economic systems and our social systems ones that actually make that possible. I think that that is possible. We believe in a world that can be just and that can be good for everyone and that can support everybody. I can't speak for the entirety of the youth across the country or across the world but I don't think that these are concepts that anyone would disagree with. I think everyone can agree that people deserve access to clean water and access to health care and access to education. Some people do, and you know that at this point some people don't have that access, and that's the kind of things that we need to fight for.

◆◆◆

I urge readers to remember that all the authors of these statements were between 12 and 19 years of age and that all of these statements were offered in the space of a webinar that lasted only an hour and a half.

The generational divide is not as wide as we might think. How could even the most cynical among us fail to be inspired by the maturity, forthrightness, honesty and clarity of the ways many youths in this country are engaging in shaping our future? Theirs is wisdom far beyond their years. They already know what many in the generations that precedes them have either forgotten or never learned: that hope is not something that someone hands you. It is something you earn. Theirs is hope founded on action that all can solidly believe in. Our leaders should take heed.

Reconciliation with One Another & the Earth
Part One: We Need Better Stories

Perhaps because I vigorously support reconciliation, I have noticed and am glad that much is being made lately of Indigenous stories and narratives as enduring cultural traditions we can all learn from. While I agree that Indigenous stories may be among the most important for us to hear right now, we should not underestimate the extent to which other stories and storytellers shape and influence our society.

While there is much we can and should learn from Indigenous storytellers, we should not ignore that fact there are other stories and ways of telling them. If they are not stories, then what are movies? That said, that we often tell ourselves the wrong kinds of stories cannot be denied. It won't be alien monsters sent by extragalactic empires seeking our precious resources, or global cabals like SPECTRE with special weapons that threaten us; it is our own paralyzing sense and habit of entitlement that will bring us down, and not just us but the entire world.

Still, though they may not be the stories we need to tell ourselves right now, it cannot be denied that their popularity continues to demonstrate our society's need for, and love of, narrative.

I think of this after listening to an interview with Margaret Atwood, ostensibly on the topic of stories and storytelling as she celebrates the publication of a new book of poems titled *Dearly* and a collection of essays called *Burning Questions*. Atwood began the interview by explaining that stories came into existence originally, not unlike songlines, to teach people what to do and not do and where to go to ensure survival. Stories also delineated the invisible, and allowed projections into the future to be made based on memories of the past and what we knew of the present. Hence, stories of rain gods and other prognostic inventions and superstitions.

But it must not be forgotten that it has always been in the nature of humans to also use stories to deceive. It did not take long for stories about enemies to emerge. These stories included warnings not just about the dangers of encounters with other species but also about the untrustworthiness of others of our own species. Stories have also been employed to evil ends. For what purpose, for example, would you keep telling stories about why you had to annually sacrifice children in order to be a good person and serve your gods? And what about stories that appeal to and justify greed and hunger for power? There have been many of these. And there are some whoppers being told now. If you don't think so, see the movie *Don't Look Up*.

As in the past, stories clearly play a huge role in our contemporary geopolitical circumstances. To hold a nation state together you need a story in which people can deeply believe. Time and again we have seen that the moment people don't believe in a common story is when things begin to fall apart. The United States is a case in point. The stories that have for more than two centuries held the United States together are those that tell of a land of virtuous light; but even that story needed an enemy – a Penguin or Joker to America's Batman, if you will. From 1945 until 1989, the Soviet Union was that enemy; an enemy that surviving Cold Warriors would like to resurrect in Putin and Russia's recent invasion of Ukraine. It won't work, of course. America's golden age has passed and whatever righteousness it thought it possessed in the eyes of the rest of the world has become suspect.

It is held widely now that the golden age did not come following the fall of the Soviet Union, because America was betrayed from within. The US itself has become an object lesson on the age-old curse of nations falling prey to the very authoritarianism that it told the world it would always protect it from.

Authoritarians, Margaret Atwood tells us, don't start out in office saying that they are going to take over and ruin your life. They inevitably start out by saying they will make things better. But Donald Trump did not make things better. The US presently appears poised to self-destruct. A divided country is wrestling over who constitutes and should constitute the real America. The bitter fight is over the very soul of the country.

As if this divisiveness were somehow contagious, the same thing is happening now in Canada. The only difference, for now, is that the stories Canadians tell themselves are different from those Americans have begun telling one another. How much longer this will be the case remains to be seen. Our democracy is under threat. O Canada! We stand on guard for thee!

Meanwhile, climate change continues to accelerate everywhere. And the story just gets worse and worse. Margaret Atwood foresees that things are going to get nastier as there is less to go around and share. One of the things that seems certain is that climate change will make food more scarce.

Authoritarianism will rise, making greater conflict inevitable. The wars brought about by climate heating will kill more people than the extreme events that warming will generate. This presents a problem for narrative, and a serious challenge to storytelling.

At present the narrative is basically that there is no future for a mid-sized, land-based, oxygen-breathing species in a world where there is less and less oxygen, which is exactly the world we will face if we kill the oceans and keep altering and heating the Earth's atmosphere.

This, I wish to submit, is not a story. Stories need characters. Statistics don't work in narrative unless they are turned into characters of the story. It isn't a story if all the narrative tells us is that we can't agree on what is wrong or what to do about it.

People feel helpless and overwhelmed. Without a guiding story, they say, how are we supposed to act? Because they don't know what to do, they don't even want to look. Instead, they simply turn away.

Margaret Atwood is right.

We need a better story.

But here we cannot but return to the lessons we might learn from Indigenous stories and storytelling. As my First Nations colleague Tim Patterson recently reminded me, as we awaken as a society to the need to commit ourselves to creating and telling ourselves new and better survival stories, perhaps we should remember the ones we have already been told.

Reconciliation with One Another & the Earth
Part Two: "All Our Relatives"

In accordance with the Charter of the United Nations and the United Nations Declaration on the Rights of Indigenous Peoples, I wish to acknowledge that *all* peoples contribute to the diversity and richness of civilizations and cultures which constitute the common heritage of humankind. And it is to the common heritage of all of humanity, past and present, that I wish to dedicate this chapter.

With that as a foundation, I would like to make an observation on the intention and potential force of the land acknowledgements that are now becoming common around the world. While this new practice is of great importance as a sign of respect, it can be, and do, even more. Land acknowledgement should be seen as more than the politics of recognizing historic territoriality. Such acknowledgement can be about more than just the past; it can also be about the present and the future. It should acknowledge the relationship between land and people. It should be about our common intention on the landscapes we share. It should be about how each of us, now, will add on a layer of experience, knowledge and narrative to the map of place.

In that context, please allow me to explain my work. The foundation of my work, and the work of the entire global water and climate community, begins with science. It seems to me that the commandments of science can be reduced to two: tell the truth and stand up for all humanity and for the planet, now and generations into the future. Good science involves not just the sharing of knowledge about the world, it is a candle we light when we want to see and be warmed by the truth. But, as the pandemic has shown us, scientific knowledge alone will not be enough to get us through the bottleneck in which we presently find ourselves on the human journey. More than at any time in history, we need to braid together all of humanity's ways of knowing and caring. We need to bring Indigenous and local wisdom as well as scientific knowledge to bear on the challenge of ensuring sustainable human presence on this planet. We cannot do that without reconciliation with one another and with the planet.

In *The Nutmeg's Curse: Parables for a Planet in Crisis*, Amitav Ghosh notes that climate change and pandemics have common causes.

Both are effects of the ever-increasing acceleration in production, extraction, consumption and environmental degradation that has occurred in the decades following the Second World War, and especially after 1989. What the pandemic has revealed is our "imperial optic," the deeply ingrained assumptions and narratives that underlie our judgment that Western ways of thinking are superior in all ways to those of others. Our Western notions of "civilizational dominance" and "infallibility," which are a legacy of colonialism, are so baked into our society as to be nearly invisible. If anything, however, what transpired during the COVID pandemic should shatter that optic. The unrest that shook America during the pandemic demonstrated, with startling clarity, how systemic societal inequalities can exacerbate the impacts of the planetary crisis. Nor was the United States the only country that discovered alarming flaws in their own perceived national character. Other nations did far better at dealing with the pandemic than many Western countries and, in so doing, put into relief just how shaky the highly divided current world order has become.

If the pandemic has any clear message, it is that no part of the world, rich or poor, will be spared by the planetary crisis – precisely because it is planetary and does not recognize borders. In Amitav Ghosh's view, it will be those who fail to see this who will be at greatest risk.

From the pandemic we also learn that inequality is a far better predictor of the likely impacts of disasters than aggregate wealth. In general, the countries that have fared the worst are those that are most inequitable: the US and Brazil, where class divisions are compounded by race; and India, with its entrenched hierarchies of caste. Over the past few decades – the very period in which the planetary crisis has been intensifying – the world's wealth has come to be concentrated in the hands of a few dozen billionaires. It could be said that neoliberal capitalism creates an illusion of wealth while picking the social fabric threadbare, so that it rips apart during disasters and climate shocks. And that widening inequality pits cooperation against forms of entitlement and individualism that turn crises into tragedies. Inequality is not just contributing to our current planetary emergency; it is virtually guaranteeing that many will not survive it. The degree of inequality we are experiencing in the midst of our current planetary crisis has deep roots.

The Mechanistic World View and Its Colonial Legacy

I am just realizing and confronting the extent to which I have been made so numb that I have denied what has been clearly before my eyes in terms of the workings of the world because of a colonial mentality that inheres so deeply, and has infected the culture of which I am part for so long, that we have come simply to live with it and accept it without so much as naming or mentioning it as a matter of historical course. Over the past weeks I have come to see how the mechanistic world view, and the manifestly unjust colonialism that we allowed to emerge from it, resides so deeply in the foundations of even my own identity that it has made it difficult to fight against. The society in which I live is so saturated with colonialism, I couldn't possibly see and understand the depth to which it, against my deepest will and intention, has, by standing in the way of truth and stifling action, made me so frustratingly helpless in confronting the very real threat of ecological and societal collapse we have sought in our collective work to prevent. But this awakening is only part of the story. I have also seen how the pursuit of science, and faith in its relentless pursuit of the truth, have delivered me to this transformation. And that, in itself, may be the larger transformation from which hope for the future will emerge for all.

Ghosh cuts deep in his condemnation of colonialism. By representing a vast continuum of human and non-human beings as "brutes," colonizers justified turning them into "resources" to be used as slaves, servants and commodities. What we are seeing now is, in his eyes, an ongoing bio-political war on an increasingly global scale that resembles the genocide of the American Indians, which included the destruction of the ecosystems upon which they relied for their existence. This genocide, and many others like it, was accompanied by an extended treaty-making process, with declarations of goodwill on all sides. Often these treaties were negotiated by people of good intention, and were signed in good faith. Yet all sides understood that the treaties, no matter how lofty their language, could and would be torn up when they clashed with what the wealthy and powerful saw as their vital interests. The resemblance of these treaties to global climate negotiations is by no means accidental. (See Appendix.)

Now, as before, the fact that the devastation is being effected by non-human "natural forces" makes it possible for many people, especially in the West – and especially in countries with settler-colonial histories – to claim that climate change is occurring entirely independently of human intentions and agency. The grounds for this claim lie precisely within the gap that modernity created between nature and culture, human and non-human. In other words, if we deny we are the cause, we can also deny colonialism.

But the fact remains that the ideologies and practices of settler colonialism have been actively promoted, in their neoliberal guise, by the world's most powerful countries, and have come to be almost universally adopted by national and global elites. It is those settler-colonial practices that are now being implemented by China, in Xinjiang; by Indonesia in Papua; and by India, in Kashmir and many of its forest regions. We have colonized not just the Americas or the East Indies, but the entire world.

This could not have been accomplished, however, without the right financial incentives. In Ghosh's view, colonialism and its attendant genocides are among the foundations of contemporary capitalism. Without the pillage of the Americas, there would be no capitalism, no industrial revolution and maybe no Anthropocene either. Ghosh makes the case that capitalism is not a given and that, in fact, with the unravelling of the mechanistic world view, its doom may now loom, adding one more dimension to the uncertainty of the current planetary crisis. But capitalism is only one of the givens in our modern industrial culture that has deep roots in colonialism.

Ghosh is also of the view that, by way of colonialism, the mechanistic world view that emerged in Europe was imposed everywhere. Modern science was used wherever colonial rule came into existence to breathe life into the view that nature was essentially inert and existed only to be exploited. The mechanistic world view went so far as to redefine how every form of life on Earth was identified and named. Blessed by empires, Linnaeus's system of taxonomy became the foundation of a way of knowing that would claim, from very early on, a monopoly on truth, discounting all other knowledge systems and their methods. Yet, secretly, Western science was often dependent on other ways of knowing.

In *Braiding Sweetgrass*, Robin Wall Kimmerer tells a story about a plant scientist who goes into the rainforest with an Indigenous guide whose ability to accurately identify various plants is so impressive that the scientist is moved to compliment him on his knowledge. "Well, young man, you certainly know the names of a lot of these plants." The guide nods and replies with downcast eyes. "Yes, I have learned the names of all the bushes, but I have yet to learn their songs."

Ghosh traces how the Linnaean system robbed rare and wonderful plants like nutmeg of their wonder and reduced them to an inert resource and, by way of colonialism, further insisted that to think otherwise – and see that wonder in them – should be viewed as child-like and fantastical – even savage – a diminishment in world view that we now see has come at considerable cost.

What may be seen as the fault here is the very idea of a single species. In fact, there may not even be such a thing. It is now known that the human body contains vast numbers of micro-organisms of various kinds; biologists estimate that 90 per cent of the human body consists of bacteria rather than human cells, and one microbiologist has suggested that under a microscope a human body looks like a coral reef, "an assemblage of lifeforms living together." It is also known that micro-organisms influence moods, emotions and the human ability to reason.

Hello! Our established idea of what a species is could be wrong. Would this not suggest, then, that we may wish to broaden the whole concept of what taxonomy means? Should it not also demand that we give new consideration to what intelligence means? If it is true that the human ability to speak, and think, can only be actualized in the presence of other species, can it really be said that these faculties belong exclusively to humans?

We see from this that even the idea of a forest far exceeds human comprehension; a name given by humans to a tree, and the forest itself, also exists as an image, and it is this that keeps it alive. In no way does this realm resemble the orderly, mechanistic universe conjured up in our society by the term "nature"; this world, in its uncanniness, is much more akin to the reality unveiled by the plague year of 2020.

But if we want to adopt a new way of thinking as a society, we had better hurry. The fires, rumours and confrontations we have witnessed at the same time we have been fighting COVID are all, in different ways, residues of human history interacting with one another in a widening spiral of catastrophe. We face a crisis that is all-pervasive and omnipresent, in which geopolitics, capitalism, climate change and racial, ethnic and religious divides interlock, each amplifying and accelerating the other. In these upheavals the residues of human history interact with non-human entities and agencies in ways that no one would have thought possible even a few years ago.

Many are now of the view that a sentient world has just about had enough of us, and wouldn't mind seeing humanity scrubbed off the surface of the Earth. Today, as we look at the floods, wildfires and droughts that afflict some of the most intensively terraformed parts of the Earth – Florida, California, the American Midwest, southeastern Australia and so on – it is hard not to wonder whether those landscapes have now decided to shrug off the forms imposed upon them by European settlers.

In any event, it is increasingly clear that the Earth can and does act, except that its actions unfold over scales of time that shrink centuries of colonialism to a mere instant, like that which separates the slipping of a boulder on a mountain slope from the landslide that follows. From that perspective, the planet may at last be responding to centuries of terraforming just as the colonial project, in its neoliberal guises, has come to be universally adopted by global elites.

These developments are making it ever more evident that many "savage" and "brutish" people understood something about landscapes and the Earth that their conquerors did not. This, perhaps, is why even hard-headed, empirically minded foresters, water experts and landscape engineers have begun to advocate policies that are based on Indigenous understandings of ecosystems. Experts even have a name, and an acronym, for this now – Traditional Ecological Knowledge (TEK). Yet the very name suggests a fundamental misunderstanding: it assumes that Indigenous understandings are usable "knowledge" rather than an awareness created and sustained by songs and stories. On this matter Ghosh concludes eloquently:

"You cannot relate to Gunung Api as the Bandanese did unless you *know* that your volcano is capable of producing meanings; you cannot relate to the Dinétah as the Diné did unless the Glittering World glitters for you too.

"The planet will never come alive for you unless your songs and stories give life to all the beings, seen and unseen, that inhabit the living Earth – Gaia."

Moving Forward

The mechanistic world view to which we have subscribed for 500 years is unravelling. Our fierce study of our own self-referential and self-justifying colonial history has upended it and the inconvenient truths it concealed. Science itself has upended its own vision of nature as machine. Every protest occurring now against inequality and ecological overshoot is an unequivocal assertion that the planetary crisis is rooted in the past and cannot be understood without it.

It is now clear that the questions of who is a brute and who is fully human, who makes meaning and who does not, lie at the core of the planetary crisis. At this moment in time, when we look back on the trajectory that has brought humanity to the brink of planetary catastrophe, we cannot but recognize that our plight is a consequence of the ways in which certain classes of humans – a small minority, in fact – have actively muted others by representing them as brutes, as creatures whose presence on Earth is solely material. It was because of these assumptions that it was taken for granted that the greater part of humanity was intellectually and culturally incapable of industrializing – and that delusion is itself an essential component of the crisis that is now unfolding across the planet.

It is perhaps only in the last two decades that the West has awakened to something that it had not imagined possible: that the non-West is fully capable of adopting extractive, carbon-intensive economies, and all that goes with them, like scientific and technical research and certain genres of art and literature. Had it been accepted earlier that all human beings are, and have always been, essentially mimetic creatures, perfectly capable of learning from one another, then perhaps sustainability would have become an urgent issue much earlier. But this possibility was precluded by long-held elite assumptions until the brutes began to unbrute themselves.

It is the tremendous acceleration brought about by the worldwide adoption of colonial methods of extraction and consumption that has driven humanity to the edge of the precipice. Half the greenhouse gases that are now in the atmosphere were emitted in the last 30 years. It is this compressed time frame that has made sure that non-humans are no longer as mute as they once were. Other beings and forces – bacteria, viruses, glaciers, forests, the jet stream – have also unmuted themselves and are now thrusting themselves so exigently on our attention that they can no longer be ignored or treated as elements of an inert Earth. Both the living and the "inert" Earth together have agency.

Surprise! The very people who were regarded as brutes and savages – the people who could see signs of vitality, life and meaning in beings of many other kinds – were right all along. The Earth teems with other beings who act, communicate, tell stories and make meaning.

So, as the mechanistic world view continues to unravel, where do we go from here?

We must rely in this planetary emergency not on billionaires, technology and geoengineering but on the proven resources of the human spirit.

To survive we have to decolonize ourselves of the deeply baked-in justification of conquest and all its related forms of genocide and extraction as inalienable elements of human nature and inevitable drivers of history. We have to wake up to the live and living world.

What does it mean to live on Earth as though it were Gaia – that is to say, a living, vital entity in which many kinds of beings tell stories? And how does the planetary crisis appear when seen from that perspective?

It is perhaps impossible to regain an intuitive feeling for the Earth's vitality once it has been lost or if it has been suppressed through education and indoctrination. Even to retrieve a sense of it from the documentary record is very difficult, because written accounts of Gaian conceptions of the world are rare – simply because those who are most powerfully aware of non-human vitality have largely been silenced, marginalized or simply exterminated by the unfolding of the very processes that lie behind the planetary crisis.

To move forward we need to recognize and transcend the increasingly obvious limitations and ideological and practical shortcomings of western elite environmentalism. What is of utmost urgency at this time is to find points of convergence on Earth-related issues between people whose concerns, approaches, life experiences and identities may otherwise be very different. While experts and scientists have a great deal to offer, this is not a project that can be left solely to the credentialed, who are by definition a tiny group of formally educated people.

A step forward would be to recognize that, as the environmental historian William Cronon has noted, there is a fundamental difference between a mere succession of events – a chronology – and a story. The difference is that the story joins events together in ways that invest them with meaning. What is really at stake is not so much storytelling itself, but rather the question of who can make meaning. Conventional wisdom has been that non-humans cannot make, or discern, meaning. If non-human voices are to be restored to their proper place, then they must be allowed to share their stories.

As they do, we may well discover again that the long-repressed vitalist instinct is universal. One does not need to be Bandanese to understand what a volcano might be to these islanders any more than one needs to be Greek to be utterly moved by *The Iliad*. It is universal empathy that makes it possible for humans to understand each other's stories: this is why storytelling needs to be at the core of a global politics of vitality.

For those who experience the Earth as Gaia, as a living, vital entity, a landscape doesn't spring to life because its inhabitants happen to share a common origin. It is, rather, the vitality of the place itself that creates commonalities between the people who dwell on it, no matter what their origin. We must see the landscapes upon which we live as being capable of making their own meaning and narrating their own stories. It is the land that makes us who we are. Not the people, the land.

"All Our Relatives"

Among the most insistently vitalist are Indigenous North American movements of resistance, which have long been based on an ethic that foregrounds the familial instinct to protect "all our relatives" – that is to say, the entire spectrum of non-human kin, including rivers, mountains, animals and the spirits of the land.

This approach is essentially spiritual or religious, yet it has been surprisingly effective. In its simplicity and power, the idea of protecting "all our relatives" may well be the key to creating bridges between people across the globe. An important indication of this lies in the many significant legal victories that

Indigenous Peoples around the world have won in recent years, precisely on vitalist grounds, by underscoring the sacredness of mountains, rivers and forests, and by highlighting the ties of kinship by which they are bound to humans.

Much, if not most, of humanity today lives as colonists once did – viewing the Earth as though it were an inert entity that exists primarily to be exploited and profited from, with the aid of technology and science. Yet even the sciences are now struggling to keep pace with the hidden forces that are manifesting themselves in climatic events of unprecedented violence. As these events intensify, they add ever greater resonance to voices that have stubbornly continued to insist that non-humans can, do and *must* speak. It is essential now, as the prospect of planetary catastrophe comes ever closer, that non-human voices be restored to our stories.

The fate of humans, and all our relatives, depends on it.

The Mother Tree Has Been Found
& Our World View Challenged

Our greatest hope may come from what science has revealed about the deeper workings of natural systems. The recent scientifically validated discovery of non-human sentience and broader intelligence in the natural world offers the greatest potential for transformation in our understanding since the rise of the ecological movement 50 years ago.

Canadian Suzanne Simard and others around the world have offered peer-reviewed research outcomes that demonstrate that trees can possess sentience and that forests can exhibit forms of intelligence over time frames until now imperceptible to humans. In this we see that Indigenous Peoples have been right all along in insisting that long-term human survival has to be predicated on an ethic that foregrounds the familial instinct to protect "all our relatives" – that is to say, the entire spectrum of non-human kin, including rivers, mountains, animals and the spirits of the land.

While some scientists remain skeptical, these findings remind us that the fact that we have not been able to plumb them does not mean there are no depths.

If science has indeed validated that trees are sentient, and that forests are intelligent, possess memory and communicate beyond the range of normal human perception over time frames incomprehensible to us, what then of other ecosystems? What epochal memories do they hold? And how can we come to share in this unfathomable knowing in time to save these systems and, in so doing, save ourselves?

I believe that we stand potentially on the threshold of the greatest reset of the dominant modern world view in 500 years. If that doesn't bolster hope for the future, nothing will.

We are on the cusp of great change. After centuries of dominance, we are on the way to replacing the mechanistic world view with one that is life affirming and based on the deep recognition of humanity's interconnectedness with the living Earth.

I am not wrong in casting Suzanne Simard as an absolute scientific iconoclast. In this observer's opinion, her ideas about cooperation, as opposed to competition, being the origin of not just sentience but intelligence in mature forests – and later in us – rank with Darwin's Theory of Natural Selection as a landmark breakthrough in Earth science thinking. How she arrived at this hypothesis also marks a breakthrough in how we should view the world. She proved to us by way of peer-reviewed science that a forest really is more than a collection of trees. Trees are, as she points out, capable of perceptiveness and responsiveness, connections and conversations. Forests really are a web of interdependence, linked by systems of underground channels, where trees perceive and connect and relate with one another by way of an elaborate filigree of roots and fungi and the millions of living things that inhabit the soil. Forests are most certainly not simply inert standing wood as forestry companies would have us believe. Forests possess an intelligence that can no longer be denied. They are wired for wisdom, sentience and healing. Our conventional wisdom is inadequate. Yes, we should be concerned about how we can save trees; but we should also be far more aware of how trees can save us.

But even concentrating on these recognitions is just skimming the surface of the deeper meaning of Simard's discoveries. And because what she has discovered is of such critical importance to us now at this moment of planetary emergency, it may be very helpful to walk the forest path she took as she explains how she came to the understandings that led to her extraordinary findings. I can almost hear her voice.

Is it possible that the trees are as perceptive of their neighbours as we are of our own thoughts and moods? Even more, are the social interactions between trees as influential on their shared reality as that of two people engaged in conversation? Can trees discern as quickly as we can? Can they continuously gauge, adjust, based on their signals and interactions, just as we do? Just as the inflection of the way Don says "Suze," and from his brief glances, I comprehend his meaning. Maybe trees relate to one another as delicately, with such attunement. Signalling as precisely as the neurons in our brains do, to make sense of the world....

Could information be transmitted across synapses in mycorrhizal networks, the same way it happens in our brains?...

Maybe I was on to something: both neural networks and mycorrhizal networks transmit information molecules across synapses. Molecules move not just across walls of adjacent plant cells and the end pores or back-to-back fungi cells, but also across the synapses of different plant roots, or different mycorrhizas. Chemicals are released into these synapses, and the information must then be transported along an electrochemical source link gradient from fungal-root tip to fungal-root tip, similar to the workings of the nervous system.

The same basic processes, it seemed to me, were occurring in the mycorrhizal fungal network as in our neural networks. Giving us that flash of brilliance when we solve a problem, or make an important decision, or align our relationships. Maybe from both networks emerge connection, communication and cohesion.

It was already accepted widely that plants use their neural-like physiology to perceive their environment. Their leaves, stems, and roots sense and comprehend their surroundings, then alter their growth, ability to forage for nutrients, photosynthetic rates, and closure rates of stomata for saving water. The fungal hyphae, too, perceive their environment and alter their architecture and physiology....

The Latin verb *intelligere* means to comprehend or perceive.

Intelligence.

Her assessment: forests can be represented as fluid intelligence.

She then goes on to blow contemporary forest management practices based on a mechanistic world view out of the water.

The trees of the next generation with genes most adaptable to change – whose parents have been shaped by a variety of climatic conditions, those attuned to the stresses of their parent, with robust defense arsenals and shots of energy – ought to be the most successful in rebounding from whatever tumult lies ahead. *The practical application – what this might mean for forest management – is that elders that survived climate changes in the past ought to be kept around because they can spread their seed into the disturbed areas and pass their genes and energy and resilience into the future. Not only a few elders, but a range of species, of many genotypes, kin and strangers, a natural mix to ensure the forest is varied and adapted.*

Of the contemporary practice of clear-cut salvage logging, she has this to say:

My wish is that we might think twice about salvage harvesting the dying Mother Trees, might be compelled to leave a portion behind to take care of the young, not merely their own but those of their neighbours too. In the wake of diebacks from droughts, beetles, budworms, and fires, the timber industry has been cutting wide swaths of the forest, the clear-cuts coalescing over whole watersheds, entire valleys mowed down. The dead trees were considered a fire risk, but more likely a convenient commodity. Great numbers of healthy neighbours have also been captured for the mills as collateral damage. This salvage cutting has been amplifying carbon emissions, changing the seasonal hydrology in watersheds and in some cases causing streams to flood their banks. With few trees left, the sediments are flowing down rivulets and into rivers already warming with climate change, harming salmon runs even further.

How can the truth of these claims be contested and ignored in the wake of the flooding that took place in the forested interior of British Columbia in November 2021? We have, as a society, clearly gone a long way down the wrong path with respect to forestry practices and there may not be time to walk back our terrible misjudgments.

Our forestry practices are self-terminating. Now that we have learned to recognize it, we know that our forests exhibit intelligence. At present, the foresters and forest companies that have taken possession of our forests are little more than forest engineers, forest miners who look at a forest and see only wood. We are knowingly wiping out other major forms of intelligence that exist on a living world we share with other sentient beings.

How can British Columbia – or any other jurisdiction for that matter – justify logging practices of this kind now that the cumulative damage they are causing is so well known? How can we permit the perpetuation of these practices when their impacts are so severe over the long term that continuing to pursue them is self-terminating for the entire forestry sector because they will put an end to the existence of forests as we have known them? When will this stop, this unravelling?

Part of the calm genius of Simard's lifework is the patient, careful, systematic way she builds up a body of peer-reviewed scientific evidence that clearly validates traditional Indigenous knowledge. The reader doesn't have to go far into the book to see that Simard is leading us there. Much of the value of the book is that Simard reports the research findings objectively, and lets the reader come to their own conclusions about what they mean.

Simard deals in the same way with the implications of the gap that exists between current forest practices and Indigenous ways of knowing and caring for the sentient world in which we all live. She leaves the reader to work that out also. It is clear, however, that escaping from the omnicidal dangers we pose to ourselves and to the rest of the world is not going to be an easy project.

What we learn from the forests and from the conventional wisdom behind the forest practices that have evolved over the past century is that in challenging a mechanistic world view that maintains that the rest of nature is just a commodity, a resource that has no being beyond utility, we should count on relentless indifference, criticism and opposition. Not enough people yet on this planet remember, are aware of or acknowledge the sentience of the living world and how that sentience supports and sustains ours. Not enough people are in a position to "go and find your own Mother Tree."

That said, like more and more of us, Simard believes that we may be in a transformational moment. Her years in the forestry profession have shown her that too many decision makers still dismiss this way of viewing nature and rely only on select parts of science. The impacts of outmoded contemporary forestry practices, however, have become too devastating to ignore. As Simard notes, "we can now compare the condition of the land where it has been torn apart, each resource treated in isolation from the rest, to where it has been cared for according to the Secwepemc principle of "we are all related," or the Salish concept of "we are all one."

Making this necessary transformation to a sustainable future – or to any livable future – requires that humans reconnect with nature – the forests, the prairie, the oceans – instead of treating everything and everyone as as an object for exploitation. It means expanding our modern ways, our epistemology and scientific methodologies, so that they can complement, build on and align with Indigenous roots. Mowing down the forests and harvesting the waters to fulfill our wildest dreams of material wealth *just because we can* has caught up to us.

What more of a breakthrough in world view do we need? We now know that cooperation as opposed to competition over millions of years allowed sentience and then intelligence to emerge in the forests as a means for them to protect and sustain themselves and all who lived in them and relied upon them. The same sentience and intelligence in the same way later emerged from cooperation in our species. It will be cooperation and not competition that, if we can generate enough of it, gets us through the climate crisis.

Examples of the value of cooperation are all around us. If we learned nothing from the COVID pandemic, the failure to put cooperation ahead of competition simply prolongs the pain of planetary crisis and only adds to the disruption of the lives of all. Only through cooperation, and the building of community, will we be able to set our world view back on course.

I believe that Simard's kind of transformative thinking is what will save us. "It is a philosophy of treating the world's creatures, its gifts, as of equal importance to us. This begins by recognizing that trees and plants have agency.

They perceive, relate, and communicate; they exercise various behaviours. They cooperate, make decisions, learn and remember – qualities we normally ascribe to sentience, wisdom, intelligence. By noting how trees, animals, and even fungi – any and all non-human species – have this agency, we can acknowledge that they deserve as much regard as we accord ourselves. We can continue pushing our earth out of balance, with greenhouse gases accelerating each year, or we can regain balance by acknowledging that if we harm one species, one forest, one lake, this ripples through the entire complex web. Mismanagement of one species is mistreatment of all."

In other words, it is time that humanity began to think like a forest.

As Simard points out, "the rest of the planet has been waiting patiently for us to figure that out."

The World Is Slowly Waking Up

Another of my Canadian colleagues, Dr. Jon O'Riordan, likes to characterize our current circumstances by quoting the opening paragraph from Charles Dickens's 1859 classic *A Tale of Two Cities.*

In his estimation of how these are "the best of times," he cites the fact that there has been a rapid growth in disruptive technologies, especially in the domains of solar and wind power generation, storage batteries and transportation efficiency. There have been breakthroughs in the understanding of natural regeneration and harnessing the power of forests, grasslands and wetlands to sequester carbon, and advances in natural climatic solutions that include regenerative agriculture.

At the same time there has been a shift toward stakeholder capitalism that focuses less on shareholder value and more on people and the planet. There is also a growing realization that we must move from self-interest to public interest or we will risk rolling societal collapse, the possibility of which can no longer be discounted. Rolling collapse would bring on "the worst of times" indeed.

There are other reasons for hope, especially over the long term. Back again here to Amitav Ghosh, who has pointed out that we, as a society, have been distracted from the full realization of the extent to which energy derived from sources like the sun, air and water could liberate us as a society. In principle every house, farm and factory could free itself from the grid by generating its own power.

While 100 per cent distributed energy is way beyond current Net Zero plans and presently beyond the capacity of even the most progressive jurisdictions in terms of imagining community-based microgrids, we should not lose sight of the benefits of aiming high with our energy transition goals.

I know it is just a dream, but imagine with me a future in which every house, farm and factory could free itself from the grid by generating its own power. No longer would power lines and gigantic, leak-prone tankers circling the world be needed for transportation of energy.

While problems associated with the increased demand for rare earths and minerals such as cobalt, lithium and vanadium for small scale battery storage would have to be overcome, there would no longer be a need for dangerous underground coal mines, or drilling rigs operating on rough seas; there would no longer be as much of a need for the long, interruptible supply chains required by the delivery of fossil fuels.

No longer would countries have to be dependent on unpredictable petro-states; no longer would they have to set aside huge portions of their annual budgets for oil payments and subsidies; no longer would they have to worry about their energy supplies being disrupted by wars with hostile neighbours or revolutions in faraway countries, and perhaps more importantly, no longer would they have to rely on superpowers to keep open the sea channels through which oil tankers must pass.

And no longer would consumers have to put up with inexplicable and utterly indefensible massive instant price hikes for fuel the moment there is any kind of disturbance in the supply chain no matter the reason and no matter where it might happen in the world.

Of course, as Amitav Ghosh points out, this would be a great disruption of the geopolitical status quo. It would mean that you don't need as much fossil fuel infrastructure and there would be no need for the corrupt power and wealth structures associated with it. The impact on the current global order could be seismic.

I know I am dreaming, but the silver lining of this terrible war in Ukraine may be, as Ghosh believes, that the liberatory potential of renewable energy and the need for a just transition away from fossil fuels will at last be fully recognized.

We face a planetary emergency. What many are saying is needed is a global treaty to phase out fossil fuels. Because climate change, like nuclear war, is an existential threat to all of humanity, the framework of a global fossil fuel treaty could be similar to treaties that have been crafted to halt nuclear proliferation. Nuclear disarmament treaties are founded on a three-stage process for making the world safer for all.

Non-proliferation > disarmament > just transition

The risks of delay are manifold. Delaying action on such a treaty will create stranded assets and the risk of financial turmoil, which will make the inevitable transition harder. Delay will slow the expansion of renewable energy and the economic diversification it promises, while at the same time allowing the powerful fossil fuel sector to continue to invisibly consolidate supportive political constituencies that oppose meaningful climate action. There is urgency here, however. As the IPCC's Assessment Review Report released in 2022 made crystal clear, we are at or near a threshold beyond which our choices with respect to climate change adaptation become ever more limited and dangerous.

The future will come to us by chance or by choice. Which shall it be?

We need to be positive – and patient. Those alive during the Industrial Revolution did not realize until a century later the significance of the changes that were wrought in their time. Similarly, it is not impossible that, because we are in the middle of a transformation, we cannot yet see its outlines.

Dealing with the threat of global heating in this climate is like trying to land a plane in a hurricane. As it happens, it falls to us – all of us who care about this planet's most vital resource, to do just that. We must fly and land the plane. It is up to us to find the words and the ways to prevent our society from falling pell-mell, every man for himself, into a future we neither planned nor desire. This can and must be our finest hour. By working together – as people and as communities – we can make it so.

The Power of Community Affirmed

The mobilization of hope is a precondition of effective action. And there is much to be hopeful about. While the recent UN global Conferences of the Parties haven't succeeded as many would have liked, global cooperation didn't collapse either. One positive thing that clearly came out of COP 26, for example, is a much greater intergenerational awareness of the seriousness of the global climate problem. This is still a time when new ideas brought forward by a new generation can have outsized impact.

Perhaps the most important thing the watching and waiting world can take away from COP 26 and its failures is that the cavalry of global climate solidarity is not coming – at least not yet – to save us. In the meantime, we are on our own in the regions in which we live, in our cities, our neighbourhoods and in our homes. This, however, should not be seen as the end of the world, only the beginning of another. Action, again, is the *sine qua non* of hope, the essential condition of hope.

In the absence of a global willingness to address the climate threat, we need to ask ourselves this question: What strategies do we need to devise on our own that will allow us to protect ourselves from extreme events and assure water security where we live?

In this context, another reason for hope is that cities are stepping up to the plate. At COP 26 in Glasgow, 1,049 cities committed to doing their share to meet emissions reduction targets on a 1.5°C trajectory. They have called their collective initiative "Cities Race to Zero." It is a challenge cities around the world are eager to meet.

If COP 26 tells us nothing else, it tells us we had better get to work to protect and save ourselves, our families, our neighborhoods and communities because it will be in them that we will have to make our stand. There is actually great power in realizing this, for it is at the local level – the level at which all of us live and work in our mountain towns – that we have the most power to effect change. And it is on that power that we need to build.

The Transformational Moment

We cannot deny that we are at a crossroads. And we are running out of time. We need to stop these wars – these heartbreaking and needless wars – get on top of this pandemic and get ahead of climate disruption before it gets ahead of us.

To do that, what we urgently need now is a second, new and very different Enlightenment. But no Enlightenment can proceed without a renaissance. We, all of us, need to be that next renaissance, to be that new and wiser beginning.

A better world is possible. To make that world possible, however, we need to harness the energy, clear-sighted intelligence and courage of our youth. Together we can be our future.

This is a transformational moment not just for Canadians but for all of us, for all of humanity. Let us seize that moment.

Mountain Towns: The Next Chapter

Perhaps more than anywhere else, this is also the midst of a transformational moment in the mountain West. This is a moment when it may be possible to create a new economic model and social fabric.

This is the moment when we can put Earth system function ahead of relentless growth as a societal priority. We now know that the high mountain regions of the world are now warming as fast as the Arctic, which is two to three times the global average. We can use how we have responded to this pandemic as a dress rehearsal for addressing the threat climate change now poses.

We can change the direction we are going in time to ensure we never come this close to the threshold of societal collapse again. We can use this moment for a global reset that will ensure a future of hope.

In making this reset positive and making it stick, the parks, protected places and natural buffer zones of the mountain West must play an expanded role in determining our future. Wilderness in the 21st century cannot simply be a place of nostalgia for what once was, but must become the seedbed for the kind of West we have yet to fully imagine. We will protect these places not just for beauty and the solace that beauty provides but because these places have the power to slow and moderate climate change. They must be crystals around which the protection, restoration and reclamation of Earth system function grow outward in surrounding communities.

From now on evolution cannot be random. It has to be conscious. Our national parks and protected places, whether they be national, provincial, regional or municipal, must be places of incubation where evolution can occur; but they must also be places where we too evolve. This must be seen as good news, for it is at the community level – where we live – that we have the greatest direct power to effect change that will make where we live a better place and positively influence the lives of those we love.

It is high time we took the justifiable fears of our children for their future seriously. Let us engage our youth who are our hope and our future and seize this moment. Together we can help what we have saved, save us. Let us seize the moment.

The West awaits its next historical age. We have to create the next best West. In order to preserve even the possibility of an enduring sense of place, Wes Jackson contends that we have to slow down our aimless, wandering pursuit of upward mobility at any cost and find a home, dig in and aim for some kind of enduring relationship with the ecological realities of the surrounding landscape. Jackson believes we have to somehow reverse the Western frontier tradition of picking up and leaving the moment a place is no longer what we want it to be. We have to learn to stop running away. We have to stay and to stand up for where we live. We have to become native again in our relationship to where we live. We have to become grounded in where we live, establish our own identities through sense of place and stand up for local values. We have to have confidence in what we are and what we can become. In this period of great change, we also have to trust in the resilience of Western landscapes and Western people.

We forget sometimes that with each decision we make and with our every action, we are making history. With each decision we make concerning the future, we are remaking our West. We should not be satisfied to simply accept what we get. We should build on our already considerable achievement by realizing the value of what we already have and have done. We should use our great success in protecting mountain places and local cultural traditions that matter to us as a crystal around which we create the West we want next. We have done it once. There is no reason we can't do it again.

What was worthwhile to the founding generations of locals in the mountain West may not exist much longer unless we take care in teaching newcomers and subsequent generations the historical lessons that took us centuries to learn. Principal among those lessons is that in this landscape our identity can never be completely defined by development. True and enduring wealth still ultimately resides, in the mountain West at least, in making peace with place, for only in so doing can we make peace with ourselves.

Is it ever too late to rejoin that great conversation between humanity and the rest of

Earthly life? No. To make that reset possible we need to find words to describe events so large they resist being pinned to the page.

In making a stand for where and how we live, we must reach into our hearts for the deepest expression of our passion for place. We must find the words for our epiphany, and then find the courage to stand by them.

Fifty years from now, a hundred years from now, and when this pandemic is merely a distant memory – when the world is likely to be even more crowded and more mobile than it is today, we will cherish even more the blank spaces on the map of the West that mean wilderness.

These landscapes will be more valuable than we can even begin to imagine today. They will be more valuable because we made them so, and because we, as Westerners, would not have them any other way.

Appendix

Six Climate Change Strategies

We find ourselves now in a different stage of the climate narrative. The sciences are not in agreement on where we go from here. According to the social sciences, presenting ever more facts at this stage may be counterproductive in terms of reaching out to the people whose minds we want to make up or change. Earth scientists worry that we are out of time and argue that we should let the weather speak for itself, let the mounting destruction speak directly to the identity and common values of those who refuse to act.

One helpful suggestion that does come from the social sciences is a preliminary breakdown of categories of public reaction to the climate threat. Helpful research recently emerging also from the neurosciences has shown why we tend to favour personal stories and shared experiences over reams of data or facts.

Neuroscientists have now demonstrated that our brainwaves actually start to synchronize and resonate with those of the storyteller our emotions are following. And that is how change of mind occurs. I laughed out loud when I read these findings. I don't have to start all over again. The principles of good interpretation – the ones by which we have stood all along – still pertain.

This is our moment. We must be the bridge between the human spirit and scientific knowledge and all other ways of knowing and caring. We need to be the embodiment of the hope the world needs and the inspiration that leads to action that will validate hope.

We have always known that to have a future, we must save the past. We must continue at all costs to protect our sense of place, and in tandem celebrate Sense of Place's magic sister, Sense of Wonder.

We know now that the best arguments in the world won't necessarily change a person's mind. What might do that, however, is a good story. We must be the keepers and tellers of unforgettable stories. Our world, however, is changing. We need to create new myths and memes that we share as part of a new era of storytelling. We need to evoke deep memories and craft them into new and compelling self-fulfilling predictions that inspire joy through meaningful action.

Each of us will have their own personal way of framing and addressing these challenges. As many readers have perhaps found, the increasing gravity of the dangerous situation we have brought upon ourselves has forced me to re-think my approaches to what I am interpreting.

I have been forced to realize that some of the approaches I've employed in the past may not work anymore.

In response, I have developed a six-point strategy for re-engaging with the problem of Earth system overshoot that has created the climate threat. I share these strategies with the aim of encouraging readers to think of theirs.

I have found that it is impossible to carry on in the midst of an accelerating period of diminishment and loss without staying focused on the wonder in the world. The best tonic for the battle-weary is a regular dose of what we are fighting to protect.

I realize now that dwelling in fresh surprises is what has always inspired me most. What has really kept me grounded in awe is new research on forests as living beings.

1. Cultivate Wonder

In *Finding the Mother Tree: Discovering the Wisdom of the Forest*, Suzanne Simard tells us that a forest is more than a collection of trees. Through careful, persistent, peer-reviewed science Simard has demonstrated that trees are, in fact, capable of perceptiveness and responsiveness, connections and conversations and that forests are a web of interdependence, linked by systems of underground channels, where they perceive and connect and relate with an ancient intricacy, and with an intelligence that can no longer be denied. Forests are not simply inert standing wood. They are wired for wisdom, sentience and healing. Simard turns conventional wisdom on its head. It is no longer all about how we can save trees. It is about how trees can save us.

By extension, this is what I have been saying for years. What we've saved, here in our mountain parks, may now save us. Simard's findings make me want to re-energize that sacred space

in my soul's innermost national park. Life talks to itself, and we can listen in. It is still possible to create cosmos out of chaos. But we need to hurry. We are witnessing a great bonfire of our heritage. Things are being lost that have not yet been found. We need to find them before they are gone. I am reawakened and thrilled. I want to begin my whole career all over again.

2. Keep Up with the Science

More than ever, I need to continue to diligently keep up with the science, with a critical expand-ed focus on changes in societal understanding and levers for action. What happened in 2021 in British Columbia was a game changer. Whether we like it or not, what is happening now in much of the rest of the world is a game changer. We have entered a new stage of climate emergency. In keeping up with the science, however, I have to be careful always not to let my feelings protect me or deflect me from the facts.

3. Undertake the Hard Work of Hope

Warnings issued by the climate science community for the past 40 years have, until now, been largely ignored. As a result, what scientists once projected to happen in the future is happening now. The future we feared and wanted at all costs to avoid has arrived, in some places 30 years earlier than anticipated. What we know at present and have projected has become like a "lantern on the stern that only shines on the waves behind us."

It is going to get worse. We must be the ones who don't lose their heads while others are losing theirs. The strategy I have used, first to navigate through the decades of public apathy with respect to action and now to come to terms with the acceleration of the climate threat, is to read, write and talk my way through it.

When I first started looking at climate change as an expression of accelerating Earth system change more than 20 years ago, it would be an exciting month if two new books

appeared on the subject. Now several appear every day. To have any grip on what my personal relationship to the climate must be if I am to have the best chance to respond meaningfully to it, I have had to recommit myself to doing the hard work hope requires: read as much and participate in as many relevant webinars as possible; write my way as much as I can to clarity of understanding and succinct expression; and rely on friends and colleagues to share what they are learning and feeling and how they are keeping positive and active. That leads me to my next strategy.

4. Find My Own Ways & Words to Tell the Story

I have found that it is one thing to have an understanding of the climate threat and how you will personally come to terms with it, and quite another to successfully communicate that understanding meaningfully to others. I am sure some of you know exactly what I mean.

When confronted with someone, perhaps even a family member, who remains unconvinced that the threat is real, you do everything you can to calmly and accurately put the case for urgent action before them – pour out your head and your heart – but to no effect at all.

It would be easy to be cynical here, and simply sit back and let the climate itself separate truth from fiction and wishful thinking with respect to the relationship between our individual identity and the common good, as happened with COVID. In the darkest moments, I imagine myself going along with the reasoning of the German health minister who glibly offered that COVID would soon resolve itself. By next spring, he said, COVID would no longer be a threat because by then everyone would have been vaccinated, cured or dead. Shouldn't we take the same approach with climate change? Shouldn't we just let floods and tornadoes convince the congenitally contrary

that not getting killed or displaced by climate disruption is actually in their interest?

Inevitably, when I stoop this low, Terry Tempest Williams comes back to remind me that anger is not an answer to evil. "Your duty, Bob," I hear her saying, "is to find the strength to bear witness and tell the truth even though it is hard to bear." I am shamed. Clearly, there is no other way forward. I have to find better ways and words to tell my story.

Then she reminds me of something that has become the foundation of my next to last strategy. "How shall we live?" she asks. "Build community," she answers. "Because in community anything is possible."

5. Build and Sustain Community

As Richard Powers observes in *The Overstory*, his amazing novel about the sentience of forests, "Life will not answer to reason. And meaning is too young to have a thing to have much power over it." As all experienced interpreters

deeply understand, there is no knowing for a fact. The path to truth is an endless one, and on that path the only dependable things are humility and looking.

We cannot do what needs to be done to face this planetary emergency alone. We need to surround ourselves with people who will help us have and share hope. We need to build and sustain community. That takes me to my final strategy.

6. Help Others Do the Same

My final strategy is to help others wherever I can to relate to and act on the climate threat in their own positive way. I am particularly committed to intergenerational dialogue and cooperation.

I want to help others explore and deepen their own sense of place and sense of wonder about the natural world; to encourage them not to fear the science and to establish their own personal relationship to concerns about

Earth system overshoot and the climate threat that has emerged from it.

I want to encourage others to find their own words and ways to express what they think and feel about the future, and to trust in and build community in the interests of that future; for it is at the local level – the level at which all of us ultimately work – that we really do have the most power to bring about change and to act most effectively in service of where and how we live and who we love, now and in the future.

Bookshelf (Works Cited)

Attenborough, David. *A Life on Our Planet: My Witness Statement and A Vision for the Future.* Grand Central, 2020.

Atwood, Margaret. *Burning Questions: Essays and Occasional Pieces, 2004–2021.* McClelland & Stewart, 2022.

Barbato, Joseph, and Lisa Weinerman (eds.). *Heart of the Land: Essays on Last Great Places.* Vintage, 1994.

Beresford-Kroeger, Diana. *The Global Forest.* Viking, 2010.

Calvino, Italo. *Invisible Cities.* Vintage Classics, 2002.

Camus, Albert. *The Plague.* Vintage International, 1948.

Ghosh, Amitav. *The Nutmeg's Curse: Parables for a Planet in Crisis.* University of Chicago Press, 2021.

Hiss, Tony. *The Experience of Place: A New Way of Looking at and Dealing With Our Radically Changing Cities and Countryside.* Knopf, 1990.

Kimmerer, Robin Wall. *Braiding Sweetgrass: Indigenous Wisdom, Scientific Knowledge, and the Teachings of Plants,* Milkweed Editions, 2013.

Legault, Stephen (ed.). *Imagine This Valley: Essays and Stories Celebrating the Bow Valley.* Rocky Mountain Books, 2016.

Lopez, Barry. *Embrace Fearlessly the Burning World.* Random House, 2022.

———. *Horizon.* Penguin Random House, 2020.

MacKinnon, J.B. *The Once and Future World: Nature As It Was, As It Is, As It Could Be.* Penguin, 2014.

Mann, Michael E. *The New Climate Water: The Fight to Take Back Our Planet*. PublicAffairs, 2021.

Moore, Kathleen Dean. *Earth's Wild Music: Celebrating and Defending the Songs of the Natural World*. Counterpoint, 2021.

Powers, Richard. *The Overstory: A Novel*. W.W. Norton, 2018.

Preston, Richard. *The Hot Zone: The Terrifying True Story of the Origins of the Ebola Virus*. Anchor Books, 1994.

Rawlence, Ben. *The Treeline: The Last Forest and the Future of Life on Earth*. St. Martin's Press, 2022.

Simard, Suzanne. *Finding the Mother Tree: Discovering the Wisdom of the Forest*. Penguin, 2021.

Solnit, Rebecca. *Hope in the Dark: Untold Histories, Wild Possibilities*, 2nd ed. Haymarket Books, 2016.

Soules, Matthew. *Icebergs, Zombies, and the Ultra-Thin: Architecture and Capitalism in the Twenty-First Century.* Princeton Architectural Press, 2021.

Stegner, Wallace. *Wolf Willow: A History, a Story, and a Memory of the Last Plains Frontier.* Viking, 1962.

White, Courtney. *The Age of Consequences: A Chronicle of Concern & Hope.* Counterpoint, 2015.

Wohlleben, Peter. *The Heartbeat of Trees: Embracing Our Ancient Bond with Forests and Nature.* Greystone, 2021.

———. *The Hidden Life of Trees: What They Feel, How They Communicate.* Greystone, 2015.

Acknowledgements

I would first like to acknowledge the extraordinary nature of the place in which I live and honour the astonishingly wise people who lived here before settlers like me arrived. I also wish to acknowledge my wife, Vi, who has always believed in this town and has worked for four decades at making it a better and better place. I would also like to thank the members of Vi's band, Vi's Guys, whose "safety meeting" discussions following jam sessions and performances have informed much of the content of this book. I also want to acknowledge the members of the Georgetown Institute, an informal think tank whose motto is "Drinkers with a thinking problem," that meets regularly

at the Georgetown Pub, for the many ideas and perspectives they have shared on the changing nature of mountain towns. I wish also to thank the members of our informal "Foreign Affairs Council," which began meeting during COVID-19 to discuss serious issues with respect to the need for societal change in the wake of the pandemic. I also want to thank my neighbours, and in particular Simon Vieyra, who for more than 25 years has both enlightened and amused me on matters related to the moral responsibilities all citizens have for the betterment of their society. I also owe a great deal of thanks to friends in the community, including real estate agents and developers, who have not shied away from talking about the challenges we face in this community. I also want to thank the weekenders, new residents, and people who have either come to work remotely or who have retired here and have not been afraid to share their stories, expectations and vision for the town. I also owe a debt of thanks to friends in

other communities for the ongoing dialogue that has allowed me to put many of the problems we face into a regional perspective. In addition, I wish to acknowledge the readers of *The Weekender Effect: Hyperdevelopment in Mountain Towns*, who continue to engage me on the issues that book put into relief. It is, in part, because of them that this sequel came into existence.

Perhaps most importantly, I want to thank my adult children, who cannot afford and do not want to live where they were born and grew up, for giving me a reason to keep caring and pressing to create a culture in Canada's western mountains that is commensurate and worthy of the landscapes that surround it.

Finally, I wish to thank Don Gorman of RMB | Rocky Mountain Books for his ongoing support for western thought and writing. I would also be sorely remiss if I didn't offer sincerest thanks to the editor of this book, Peter Enman, who contributed greatly to its or-

ganization and clarity. And last, but certainly not least, I want to thank Chyla Cardinal and Gerilee McBride, book designers par excellence, for the work they have done to make this book presentable. I thank you all!